EQUIPPED FOR VICTORY

EQUIPPED FOR VICTORY

YINKA AKINTUNDE

**RESOURCE HOUSE LTD
LONDON**

Copyright@ Yinka Akintunde 2010

All Rights Reserved

ISBN : 978-0-9755140-7-8

No part of this book may be reproduced in any form by photocopying or by any electronic or mechanical means, including information storage or retrieval systems without permission in writing from both the copyright owner and the publisher of this book.

First Published 2010 by
RESOURCE HOUSE LTD
P O BOX 944
Dagenham
RM9 9JW
United Kingdom

All Bible quotations have been taken from the New King James Version of the Bible, unless otherwise indicated in the text. 'KJV' refers to King James Version. 'Amp' refers to Amplified bible. 'NIV' refers to New International Version. 'NLT' refers to New Living Translation.

Printed for Resource House

Table of Content

Chapter 1 : Warring Breed, Winning Breed........01

Chapter 2 : Belt For Your Loin...........................17

Chapter 3 : The Body Armour.........................55

Chapter 4 : Good News, Good Steps..................69

Chapter 5 : The Sword Of The Spirit.................83

Chapter 6 : Sheild Those Darts Off....................105

Chapter 7 : Under Divine Covering.....................149

Chapter 8 : Prayer Is In Your Armour.................163

Chapter 9 : He That Wars................................203

INTRODUCTION

Personal battles are the mother of all battles. They are the ultimate in the world of wars. Mankind has been fighting wars from time immemorial, but no war can be compared to personal battles. Some of the costliest wars fought in history have been avoidable, some were unnecessary while many were uncalled for. As for personal battles, they are not optional. You do not need to challenge for the battle. Minding your own business does not exempt you from one. Personal battles are never resolved amicably; no peaceful resolution is strong enough to avert them. They are must-fight battles to win or lose and are the platforms of life's victory or vanquish. There is no draw in the battles of life. You either prevail or the challenging force prevails.

The first mistake a Christian can make is to think that there is no war going on. The scripture clearly says that we are at war, and our only aim and intention is to win and subjugate the challenging force.

For though we walk in the flesh, we do not war according to the flesh; for the weapons of our warfare are not carnal but mighty in God for pulling down strongholds, casting down arguments and every high thing that exalts itself against the knowledge of God, bringing every thought into captivity to the obedience of Christ, and being ready to punish all disobedience when your obedience is fulfilled…2 Corinthians 10:3-6

CHAPTER 01

WARRING BREED, WINNING BREED.

The kingdom of darkness would be out of type to just let you go about winning in life without mounting any challenge, having had you in their custody for years before coming into light. No matter how early in life you became born-again, you still were in the camp and kingdom of darkness once upon a time, no matter how morally upright you were in the kingdom of darkness before. Essentially the battle the enemy is fighting with you is that of jealousy because you changed address and position.

Giving thanks to the Father who has qualified us to be partakers of the inheritance of the saints in the light. He has delivered us from the power of darkness and conveyed us into the kingdom of the Son of His love, in whom we have redemption

through His blood, the forgiveness of sins…Colossians 1:12-14.

If you are worthless and down already, you need no fear of falling. I mean if your past, present, and future, and even the entirety of your destiny is worthless, the enemy will not bother about you. But alas, you are a heavy cargo, a worthy citizen of God's kingdom. Many destinies are tied to your own. You are the extension of God's saving arm on the earth, and things are tasteless without you. Evil resistance, therefore, is not strange to your status assignment and mission, but you must win. No one goes into a battle they do not want to win. No matter how ill-equipped, unprepared, or even incompetent a warrior is compared to the enemy at hand, everyone charges to the battle with the singular intent and desire to win. The sad reality is intent and desire, as good and strong as they may be, are not enough in prosecuting a successful warfare in life.

Personal battles are fought on different fronts against diverse' foes, but the ultimate is the battle against the wiles of the devil. So crucial and fierce is this battle that God has to lend you his own armour for you to successfully prosecute the war and win. There is no good parent who wants his or her ward to lose any battle, no matter how trivial. What will one gain in seeing his son or daughter broken, beaten, and battered in front of their foe? God is not ready to see you beaten and battered over and again by the adversary, so he made available his armour unto you. The weapon of warfare made available by the Almighty God is indeed mighty, enough to pull down any challenge. We were told that Goliath of Gath, whom David killed, was a giant. So was his amour, but David had God's weapon. Goliath could not have been taller than God, no matter how tall he was. No wonder he came down once someone showed up with God's very armour. A stone could not have killed a giant of Goliath's stature, experience, and expertise. God did through his amour in David's hand. You are given the mighty weapon of the Almighty God in life's battle. No battle should be too big to conquer for you!

In fact, you are made for the tough ones. No nation fights little burglars with armoured tanks, missiles, and big artilleries. Friend, stop magnifying what you are going through. You have armouries mighty enough for any size of battle you are fighting.

All you need is to get them engaged.
You shall win.

Finally, my brethren, be strong in the Lord, and in the power of his might. Put on the whole armour of God, that ye may be able to stand against the wiles of the devil…Ephesians 6:10-11

I love the word "finally," which means no matter how much you might have done or put in place in life, after all the university degrees, the motivational speeches, after all the strategies put in place as human, victory in life's battles can still only be guaranteed on the platform of divine armour. Thank God he did not give you man's armour but his very own amour to fight life's battles. Man's armour is not sufficient for dealing with the wiles of the devil. If God were to be a man here on earth, the very amour He would have used in fight is what he had made available for you in his wisdom and kindness. I hope you know God is a veteran who does not lose out in battle. The Lord of host is his name. **Psalm 24:7-10.**

Jesus came to earth and demonstrated how to engage the Father's armour, and lo in three and half years, he was so victorious that the news of his triumph is still fresh and proclaimed daily thousands of years later. He took the battle to the enemy's gate and rubbed his nose on the floor. Hence you are qualified for victory in all areas of your life too.

Having wiped out the handwriting of requirements that was against us, which was contrary to us. And He has taken it out of the way, having nailed it to the cross. Having disarmed principalities and powers, He made a public spectacle of them, triumphing over them in it…Colossians 2:14-15

God's armour is spiritual, meant for the man of the spirit to engage in first. Then the fruits of victory will start showing in the outer man. Our weapon of warfare does not put us in a negotiating position with the enemy. God's armour puts us in a vantage place in the spirit realm so we can pull down the strong holds, no matter how strong they are holding up against you.

Strongholds are barriers, limitations and fortress erected against your progress. Holds are an array of forces that set themselves in your way to deny you the freedom and victory bought for you through the bruising, beating, crucifixion, burial, and resurrection of Jesus. You are not to treat them with kid gloves. You are to pull them down. The good news is that no matter how strong the holds are, they will come down. All you need to do is to pull them using the weapon of warfare made available for you in God through Christ Jesus.

You are actually a specialist, by virtue of your new birth, in dealing with difficult issues. Serious issues may call for a bitter cry at times, but a bitter cry will not create the necessary damage to the issues troubling you. It will make them look greater than they are and will not solve the problem either. Many in the world today have the gift of diagnosing, analysing, and magnifying problems, but only few proffer solutions or engage the problems to obtain the desired result. I hereby come to you through this book as a messenger of God, sent to show you the way out in dealing with serious issues.

When serious issues rise up against a believer, the common question people ask is "why?" The why is because you are the bearer of the knowledge of God on Earth. **2Corinthians 10:5b.**

Whenever satanic machination (imagination) and those great things that seem insurmountable stand up against you, the target of the enemy is the knowledge of God in you. The target is not your money even though the challenges may manifest in your finances. The target is not your children, husband, or wife even though the challenges you are seeing now may be in your family life. The target is not your physical body even though there is a health issue. The enemy is set out to make the knowledge of God in you ineffective. When Satan set his evil imagination against humanity in Eden, and pitched his strong hold against the family of Mr. and Mrs. Adam, what he went for first was the knowledge of God in them. **Genesis 3:1-6.**

The backbone of the conversation in Eden between the serpent and the woman primarily involved questioning and denials of God's love and care, his promises and provisions for Adam household. Eve fell for it and they were stripped of glory. Satan said, if God really cared as he appeared to, he would have not only made you realize the benefits of eating the tree of knowledge of good and evil he wouldn't also have placed restriction on it. Satan was not going to marry Eve if they had broken up. Neither was he going to live in Eden if they were chased out. All that the enemy of their soul was interested in was the knowledge of God in them.

The same trick was tried on Jesus on Earth but he prevailed over the wiles of the devil, **Luke 4:1-13.** No wonder Jesus was boldly proclaimed as the worthy triumphant Christ!

Then I saw a strong angel proclaiming with a loud voice, "Who is worthy to open the scroll and to loose its seals?" And no one in heaven or on the

earth or under the earth was able to open the scroll, or to look at it. So I wept much, because no one was found worthy to open and read the scroll, or to look at it. But one of the elders said to me, "Do not weep. Behold, the Lion of the tribe of Judah, the Root of David, has prevailed to open the scroll and to loose its seven seals…Revelation 5:2-5.

Anytime challenges and the seemingly high things of life rise up against you, have it in the back of your mind that the battle is against the knowledge of God in you. All troubles in a believer's life are a direct affront to the love and will, purpose, promises, and provision of God. The enemy is out to prove that what God has already done through Christ was not real. He is out to prove that divine agenda does not exist and if there is anything at all like that, it is not in your best interest. That devil is a liar. Divine agenda is in your best interest. This is why God is not leaving it to you all by yourself. God calls your life battles His battle as well. He is involved and will see to it that you win. You do not have to be gentlemanly or whimper at life's affairs. No, you need to stand tall and be ready to avenge satanic affront in all ways and at all levels. **2 Corinthians 10:6.**

Divine weapons for your triumph in life's warfare are not vague. They are not nebulous. They are real, tangible, and useable. You are a spirit being so you have the capacity to lay hold of spiritual weapons. God's weapons are spiritual weapons, for God is a spirit. Employing the force of the flesh in engaging the weapon of the spirit will end up in frustration and a great one, for that matter. You need to know how to position your spirit in handling what God had made available for us in Christ Jesus as your weapon of triumph. Real life battles are not battles against your neighbour or your boss. They are not battles against folks who do not share the same religious perspective or convictions as you. Life battles are not against the other tribe, ethnicity or nation. All the warfare of life is against spiritual entities. It is not necessarily the truth that a demon is fighting against you whenever things go wrong. But the reality is that things go wrong because the kingdom of darkness still has a legal hold of manipulation on this world system as long as at least one person who is not yet redeemed into God's kingdom still lives on earth thereby representing the first Adam who gave the authority of life on Earth unto the devil.

God's kingdom came truly, as the apostles were asked to pray, after Jesus' resurrection, but it only comes to individuals who, by choice, make Jesus, the Son of God, their Lord and King. **Luke 17:21.**

As the number of the kingdom carriers increases through new birth, God's kingdom is growing and becoming established on earth. This will continue until Jesus returns to finally flush out the devil and his kingdom at the end of time. Until then, we still live in a world essentially subject to the evil manipulation of the wicked one, so you need personal triumph to enjoy personal victory on this side of eternity.

If we war against spirit, it is unwise to fight spirit with flesh. Your spirit man is the valid warrior you need to engage in pulling down the stronghold of darkness. In fact, life's ultimate battles are not fought against the might of the devil. A monster with two horns and stinging tail or biting tongue is out of question in the reality of life's battle. The ultimate battles are against the "wiles" of the devil.

Same War, Different Battles

The thief cometh not, but for to steal, and to kill, and to destroy: I am come that they might have life, and that they might have it more abundantly…
John 10:10

The Lord Jesus made it clear here that the devil is not just a thief but "the thief", which means all other thieves and destroyers take their source authority and strategies from him.

Moving from Africa to Europe, I transitioned from a region where religion and the things of the spirit are taken seriously and most times even to unprofitable and unreasonable or many times uncomfortable extremes. I moved to a region where less attention is paid to such things. I moved to a region where Christianity and spiritual things are largely regarded as mere geographical, historical, and archaic issues given attention by some myopic ones. I started asking questions why evil seems to prevail in my own former part of the world, despite the massive religious activities, than where God has been relegated to an infinite and seemingly irrelevant background. One can even be tempted to start thinking that if the devil truly is behind all evil he must have vacated the west and moved to other parts of the world, especially when one considers the prevalence of poverty and squalor in the midst of plenty as a result of wicked leadership and bad followership compared to the abundance of good roads, plentiful food, and good things of life in the west. But having lived in both worlds, I realised that evil is as rife in the west as it is in other parts of the world. The shade and colour of manifestation is the only difference.

To kill, steal, and destroy lives and destiny is the devil's only mission. He is referred to as "the thief," and he will undertake his mission through poverty in the under developed world as much as he would do it with extreme and wild craving for pleasure in the developed world. For the devil, the end is what justifies the means - narcotics addiction and lethal overdoses in London, United Kingdom or tuberculosis not properly prevented or managed in Lagos, Nigeria are for the same purpose and to achieve the same goal. Gender suppression in the ignorant world of the uneducated Afro-Asian or divorce made easy in the trendy professional modern world of New York means the same to the enemy. As long as homes are broken and family institutions are ripped apart, hearts and lives are broken with posterity put in jeopardy. So long as children's security is compromised, disgruntled and hurt kids thrown to the dark world of the street at the mercy of barons and pimps, the thief is satisfied with his mission accomplished. Killing with guns in the jungle of Mexico or voodoo at the back side of Africa, hatred in the office, or diplomatic war at the global front, as long as lives, visions, dreams, and destinies are killed, stolen, and destroyed, the devil is satisfied. We may narrowly assume and stigmatise a part of the world as crude and unsafe, but the larger picture shows us a rather crude and unsafe world all over.

The mind of man is a gift from God and is the channel of all innovations on Earth. Every good and lofty invention needed to make life good and sweet on Earth will only come through the instrument of people's minds. Even when people are inspired through the spirit, the interpretations and applications here on Earth are mind products. Democracy itself is not a guarantee of good governance and good life, but when good leaders with good will in their mind rule, progress is made and humanity blessed whatever the brand. Citizens of many nations of the world suffer unnecessary hardship today not because of the system of government but because of the wickedness in the minds of the leaders, past or present.

When good people run things, everyone is glad, but when the ruler is bad, everyone groans. Proverbs 29:2. (The Message)

Wars are fought because of evil ambitions and intentions in the minds of leaders. Aircraft, medicines, good roads, warm shelter, good food, and all other good things of life are products of the human mind at work. Evil and good have their fountain in man's mind and that is why the devil bombards man with wiles to twist the mind.

For example, while the devil bombards some in their minds to be lazy, never thinking, always looking up to heaven for manna, expecting God to sort out everything for them, he likewise bombards others to see no need for God as long as there is science and the rule of law. We thereby see two extreme ends of deceit- one is suffering, ever poor, never advancing while the other end is comfortable, and innovative but idolatrous and self worshiping. One extreme makes living a hell on Earth a career and the criteria for going to heaven. The other makes this Earth their own heaven and sees no need to either go or even believe in heaven beyond here and now again. One passes all his human responsibility to God thereby doing nothing. The other is doing everything to prove that there is no God or even if there is a God, what is he needed for. No matter how or where the battle is fought, as long as the life and destiny of mankind is killed, stolen, and destroyed, whether in temporal or eternal sense, the devil's mission is accomplished.

War Of Wiles

You are of your father the devil, and the desires of your father you want to do. He was a murderer from the beginning, and does not stand in the truth, because there is no truth in him. When he

speaks a lie, he speaks from his own resources, for he is a liar and the father of it …John 8:44

The word "lie" here is same as "wiles" in Ephesians 6:11. This is to show us how the devil accomplishes his notorious missions of killing, stealing, or destroying. The same wile that makes someone steal money meant for a whole nation while children are dying of sicknesses and malnutrition is the same wile that stirs up lust in the mind of an adult to abuse hapless children in their care and exploits them for inordinate affection and evil pleasure in any guise. Personal battles are majorly against the wiles of the devil. It takes the armour of light to dispel and disarm the kingdom of darkness.

We are not only meant to know and appreciate the components of the armour of God. We also need to know that the armour delivers only when the components come together like a jigsaw and are properly engaged day in, day out. No wonder the Bible did not talk of armours, but the whole armour. When a component is missing, the fighter is vulnerable. It is not yet armour until it is complete. Most casualties we suffer in life's battle are traceable to the fact that saints are holding on to some components of the armour while indifferent or negligent to or even ignorant about the others. Yet the Bible said the whole armour is needed in order to be able to stand the onslaught of the enemy. Each component is made against a specific wile or wiles of the devil. The whole armour is for the whole victory package. The scripture clearly shows that you will be able to stand your ground any day against any form of evil when your amour is in full use. Not only will you stand firm, you will be the last one standing because everything standing against you will be grounded for you.

God specifically choose the armour components because he knows what the devil has in his arsenal, God did not bother to include a component for any weapon the devil will not bring your way. The sad irony is that many times, saints are busy carrying self-made armour against weapons they perceive the enemy has while leaving the ones recommended by the all knowing God behind. Like your father, you ought to be the one in the know of the strength strategies and limitation of the enemy you are dealing with.

Lest Satan should get an advantage of us: for we are not ignorant of his devices…2 Corinthians 2:11

The Bible here is not advising us or praying for us to be aware of the devil's devices. The apostle was making an affirmative statement that they did know the devices of the devil, and they are taking the right steps not to be taken advantage of by him. As a believer, you should be in the know, not just the pastors or apostles. Here the apostle used the word "we", which included the people he was writing the epistle to, as not being ignorant of the devices of the devil, which are wiles or lies. The idea of the devil many believers are carrying around is rooted in what they were told as unbeliever, saw in a movie, or read in a comic, which are always wrong and presumptuous. The only authentic light that accurately exposes all works of darkness is the word of God.

Having therefore established the fact that the ultimate battles are personal, we must win with God's amour against the wiles of the devil. I need to then say that God is not going to equip but has already equipped you. He is not going to provide but has provided you with the needed armour. The responsibility is now in your hand to arrange the puzzle and put the armour on for a good fight.

My assignment in this book is to help you see, pick up, and put on that which has been made available to you in Christ, that you may by them wage a good warfare in life.

You are winning all the way in the mighty name of Jesus. Amen.

Yinka Akintunde

CHAPTER 02

BELT FOR YOUR LOIN

The whole armour matter starts here. Strangely, no one dressing up starts with the belt, but funny enough, it is not a mistake that the belt of truth comes first in the armour series. Every fabric and fibre of the other components draws value from this part. As the devil's arsenal is built on and around lies, therefore Jesus called Satan the father of lies, so is the arsenal of light built on truth.

When life's business becomes serious, you need the belt of truth. This was demonstrated for us when Jesus was prepared to go to the cross. He needed to drive home some issues while washing the disciples' feet, so he girded his waist and went about the business at hand. The belt's purpose originally was to secure the skirt or trouser and not a mere fashion accessory as it is today. So it is with truth.

The truth is not another fashion "bling" in your Christian armour. It is the belt to secure your garment and keep your veil of glory intact on you. Just as the purpose of the belt is primarily to hold fast the trousers lest the wearer get stripped and lose their pride, honour and dignity, the belt of truth helps us keep in place the honour and dignity that accompany salvation.

The loin in question here is the loin of your heart. Every battle of life has at least a front in the heart or mind. Even physical wars create fear, hatred and despair in the hearts or minds of men naturally to say the least. Since we war not against a physical entity principally, the heart or the mind, therefore, becomes the main target of the adversary whenever you are facing challenges in any area of life. The need could be in your pocket, but the real pain is felt in the heart. The divorce may be done on paper, but the separation is seated in the heart. People can murder with their hand or mouth, but the hatred that birthed the action is always rooted in the heart. Racism is not about the colouration of sight but of the mind. Prejudice is the reaction of the heart or mind to past experience or information about an idea or people. At worse, it is the wrong judgment of others the mind refuses to let go or change even when it is contrary to reason.

Wars of immense costs and significant consequences have been fought in different parts of the world based on this misconception in the human mind. The truth is, before a bullet was fired on ground, millions of cannons had been loaded in the hearts of men, which is the real battle ground. The word of God admonished us to guard our hearts or loins with diligence. This guarding can only be done with belt of truth.

Keep thy heart with all diligence; for out of it are the issues of life...Proverbs 4:23

The palace guard which was ordained by God to keep your heart or loin is the belt of truth. Once you are saved, the fountain of life takes residence in your inner man. The source of abundant life is your spirit; the pumping machine is your heart or mind while your tongue is one of the channels of the flow. The channel only delivers what is issued from the fountain.

God is not the only one interested in making your heart his depot of life. Satan is also interested in making it a depot of death. It is your duty to therefore guard your heart or loin with the truth so that when the enemy comes like a flood, the army of truth you guard your loin with will keep you safe. This is the reason the Bible talks of life and death being in the power of the tongue, and you know the tongue is just a servant, a channel for the expression of what is issued from the fountain, for out of the abundance of the heart the mouth speaks.

Christ will not come down and die for you again to conquer death. He has done it already - **Hebrew 2:13**. He will not be beaten again for your healing, for he has already been beaten once and for all - **Isaiah 53:5**. He is not going to be made poor again. He was made poor once and for all - **2 Corinthians 8:9**. Whenever there are challenges in your life manifesting in contrary dimension to what has been done and accomplished for you in Christ Jesus, your spirit must lay hold of the truth concerning such issue like a deed of purchase and pitch a tent therein without compromise. For example, when you are born again, you have been born into the family of God and of the lineage of the blessed Abraham. This supersedes any natural lineage you were born or adopted into. If the first covenant of your natural birth is enough, there will not be any need for the new birth. But the new birth came to help you fix the old one in case there is a problem therein. Hallelujah!

And if ye be Christ's, then are ye Abraham's seed, and heirs according to the promise…Galatians 3:16

No matter how dysfunctional your natural family was, you have been re-born, adopted, and received into the beloved. Just like your natural family is your blood family, your spiritual family is much more a blood family also, knowing full well that the shed blood of the Lamb of God (Jesus Christ) was your inroad and link with the family of God.

Blessed be the God and Father of our Lord Jesus Christ, who hath blessed us with all spiritual blessings in heavenly places in Christ: According as he hath chosen us in him before the foundation of the world, that we should be holy and without blame before him in love: Having predestined us unto the adoption of children by Jesus Christ to

himself, according to the good pleasure of his will, To the praise of the glory of his grace, wherein he hath made us accepted in the beloved. In whom we have redemption through his blood, the forgiveness of sins, according to the riches of his grace...Ephesians 1:3-7

You can then boldly say that you have a goodly heritage, a blessed lineage. This is the belt you need to keep your blessed family garment on every time the devil comes with wiles trying to impose all sort of evil trends on you in the name of ancestral curses, family sickness, lineage disease and problem. The belt of truth is what the Spirit of God living in you uses in setting the standard as to where the trousers stay when the enemy comes like a flood to strip you of that which you have been freely given as inheritance in God through Christ. No inheritance or destiny is secure in Christ beyond how firm or tight you hold it with the belt of truth. God in his word is saying he cannot help you hold it. All he will do is to make his truth available unto you. It is your responsibility and duty to make a belt out of the truth to hold your inheritance and destiny. No wonder Christ said, when men know the truth, the truth will make free men out of them.

And ye shall know the truth, and the truth shall make you free...John 8:32

The truth as seen here never talked about setting you free but making you free, making a free man who cannot be bound of you. We often think these scripture talks of you being bound and then getting set free by the truth, but that is not the whole truth. The truth is not meant to set free but to make you free, and these are not same and equal. God's ultimate plan is to make you a man who cannot be fettered, no matter how hard the enemy tries rather than someone to be set free now and then when bound by the enemy.

Believers are busy running around looking for anointing that removes or breaks the yoke, so to speak, and it is sad to see preachers make this the daily dose believers are fed. They need to always come back to them for yoke destruction and burden removal thereby creating a perpetually sick dependent, ever-bound customer of saints. The question you start asking is how often these folks get yoke. If the anointing removes and destroys yokes and burdens, once you are set free, ought you not to remain free seeing that he who the Son sets free is expected to be free indeed? The sad truth is that many are set free by the anointing but they are not made free by the truth, so they have to go back for repeat episode as often as possible. This is not the will of God for us in Christ Jesus.

Christ Jesus sets us free or snatches us from the kingdom of darkness by the reason of his death, burial, and resurrection whenever we receive him into our life.

So if the Son sets you free, you are truly free ...John 8:36

Being set free is not a guarantee that freedom will be

enjoyed. The one who binds is still roaming about like a lion looking for those to bind in one form of darkness or the other. So what Christ does to seal your freedom is to reveal his truth to you. It is this truth that will now make a free man not subject to bondage again out of you. So, salvation and anointing, no matter how mighty it flows, can only set a man free. It takes the truth to make a free man out of him. This simple equation is the reason why many go through endless deliverance sessions and yet they are fettered, prayed for, but still in bondage. It is possible to be saved and not enjoy the liberty that is in Christ Jesus, married to Christ the head of all principalities and power and yet be talking about and living in the fear of "spirit husbands and wives".

What Is The Truth...Eternal Realities.

We often equate things to truth because they have been on ground and believed to be true for a long time. Often we equate our experiences or that of others to the truth thereby making all effort and argument in conforming the truth to our experience instead of doing otherwise. This is the sure way of proliferating errors in the body of Christ.

Truth is the revelation of eternal realities. It is not affected by time or season. The level of revelation permitted and bearable by humanity at a given time does not change the truth. Still, neither do the facts at hand change it.

When Jesus was on Earth, some of the facts accepted as the truth till then were eventually described by the Lord as changeable facts born out of bearable revelations, but the truth remained constant in God.

Some Pharisees came to him to test him. They asked, "Is it lawful for a man to divorce his wife for any and every reason?" Haven't you read," he replied, "that at the beginning the Creator 'made them male and female, and said, 'For this reason a man will leave his father and mother and be united to his wife, and the two will become one flesh' ? So they are no longer two, but one. Therefore what God has joined together, let man not separate." "Why then," they asked, "did Moses command that a man give his wife a certificate of divorce and send her away?" Jesus replied, "Moses permitted you to divorce your wives because your hearts were hard. But it was not this way from the beginning. I tell you that anyone who divorces his wife, except for marital unfaithfulness, and marries another woman commits adultery."...Mathew 19: 3-8

Here we see Jesus separating the obtainable and bearable facts on ground, which are subject to time, season, and dispensations, from the truth that is eternal. Many would have built their businesses, marriages, and entire lives on those facts taken for truth, which would still be alright based on what had been revealed to mankind then. But to have assumed there was nothing more to life in God beyond what they had then was what robbed many of the victories God had for them in destiny. Facts can be changed when truth is established. The poor can become rich, sick become healed, bitter turned sweet, weak made strong, and sinner turned to saint when truth finds its rightful place. Change happens when truth displaces facts no matter how long it's been on ground.

Victory in life is a desired effect of change - change from victim to victor, from being hunted to being the hunter, from being devoured to becoming the evil destroyer are not just desirable but obtainable.

Facts displacement by truth guarantees your change from being chased around to being the one chasing evil away and chased by goodness and mercy all the days of your life. This is why Jesus said that the ultimate delight of God the father is that his people enter into the fullness of reality (truth) and make such reality the platform of their relationship with him (worship) as they perpetuate the fellowship with his Spirit through their spirit.

So Jesus made this profound statement:

God is spirit and his worshipers must worship in spirit and in truth...John 4:24

The truth is that eternal reality which is always consistent with God's perfect will as revealed in his purpose, plan, promises, and provisions for us through Christ Jesus. Truth, therefore, is not a mere agglomeration of facts but a revelation of realities.

These realities, seen or unseen, are consistent even when facts change position. For example, the truth is that God loves everyone equally no matter how bad or good they are.

The fact is this, some will still perish based on their response or lack of it to this offer and the response being personal, and varies from one person to another.

For God so loved the world that He gave His only begotten Son, that whoever believes in Him should not perish but have everlasting life. John3:16

Even though the fact shifts ground from one person to the other, the truth or eternal reality is still the same. God does not want anyone to perish.

Therefore I exhort first of all that supplications, prayers, intercessions, and giving of thanks be made for all men, for kings and all who are in authority, that we may lead a quiet and peaceable life in all godliness and reverence. For this is good and acceptable in the sight of God our Saviour, who desires all men to be saved and to come to the knowledge of the truth…1Timothy 2:1-4.

Whether in the Old or New Testament, the truth is a constant. It does not change. The revelation of the truth took place over time and dispensations were gradually exposed from Adam to Noah, from Abraham to Moses, David and the prophet. When Christ came on the scene, he epitomized the fullness and ultimate revelation of the truth. He also became the access and guarantee of access to the truth for mankind.

In content, not all statements in the Bible represent the truth, even though the Bible is the book of truth. Some statements made were the reflection of the mindset of the speaker and not God. That is why the whole scripture was inspired by God so that the truth will eventually be revealed and God's mind known to us in context beyond mere letter. Abraham, Moses, Elijah, Elisha, David, and all great men of God in the Old Testament were indeed great and good examples of walking with God in one dimension of life or the other, but none of them fully represented the full expression of the truth. So it is dangerous to follow these men hook, line and sinker as a new testament Christian. This is where many Christians get it wrong. Many want other human beings to fall so that they can rise, but it does not work that way in Christ. Many preachers do not have a message apart from pulling other ministries down, saying they are the Elijah and Jeremiah of our age as they fight over doctrines and traditions. Neither Elijah nor Jeremiah epitomised an example of the New Testament ministry.

In Christ Jesus, love as an issue is the ultimate and even stronger than being right in theology.

For in Christ Jesus neither circumcision nor uncircumcision avails anything, but faith working through love... Galatians 5:6

The truth is good news. Anything contrary to good in the news is not the truth. Many things preached to believers only rob them of their confidence, strip them of their covering in Christ, and deny them of seeing the reality of what has been done already in Christ Jesus. When people are fed on ideas based on someone's experience while in darkness and half-baked truth, the wholesomeness of the truth is jeopardized. The Bible as the word of truth will only deliver what it carries, when it is rightly divided. It is easier to spot blatant heresies or apostasy than wrongly divided word. No wonder the scripture admonished you to be diligent with the word so that the truth can be rightly divided. It is the only way out of shame of defeat.

Be diligent to present yourself approved to God, a worker who does not need to be ashamed, rightly dividing the word of truth... 2 Timothy2:15.

When people go into heresy or apostasy, it is easy to deal with knowing that such has stepped out of the house, but when people are wrongly dividing the word of truth, they are inside yet not covered. They are prone to all molestations and harassment suffered by those who are outside. To know what the word says is not enough as truth but the right interpretation of it in the context of God's will. This is referred to as rightly dividing the word of truth.

Accessing The Truth

Talking about the belt of truth, we are looking at truth from God's perspective, truth through God's lenses, not just mere empiricism. We thereby see the Bible as not just a compilation of stories, geographical facts, and figures or mere tenets of a religion. We see the Bible as God's "given book."

All scripture is given by inspiration of God, and is profitable for doctrine, for reproof, for correction, for instruction in righteousness: That the man of God may be perfect, thoroughly furnished unto all good works...2 Timothy3:16-17.

The man of God here simply refers to the man who has something to do with God, the man who is interested in what God has to say. Though there are many books, different authors, and various chapters making up the content, in context the scripture is a singular book. It is just a book given through inspiration aimed at a singular purpose of revealing the very heart of God to his people thereby removing imperfections and furnishing them thoroughly with good things needed in the journey of life towards a good end.

If the scripture is given, it will take the revelation from the giver for the truth to be grasped. Until the truth is revealed, the profit in the scripture cannot be delivered.

The secret things belong unto the LORD our God: but those things which are revealed belong unto us

and to our children for ever, that we may do all the words of this law...Deuteronomy 29:29.

Even though they were given the book of the law, we can see from the above scripture that it would take revelation for the words therein to be relevant to them, knowing fully that the doing of the truth (word) is what places value on the truth. For this they need revelation. You do not need revelation to argue or debate about the scripture. Paul did not need revelation to argue and debate the scripture as Saul. He argued so much that he started seeing to it that dissenting voices were eliminated. He brought his religious experience and intellectual proficiency, being a lawyer, into fore in his argument yet he got everything right except the truth.

For ye have heard of my conversation in time past in the Jews' religion, how that beyond measure I persecuted the church of God, and wasted it: And profited in the Jews' religion above many my equals in mine own nation, being more exceedingly zealous of the traditions of my fathers. But when it pleased God, who separated me from my mother's womb, and called me by his grace, To reveal his Son in me, that I might preach him among the heathen; immediately I conferred not with flesh and blood...Galatians 1:13-16

The difference between Saul the persecutor and Paul the ambassador was revelation. The revelation of the truth to him by God made a free man out of him and changed his status forever. Whatever murderous devil was indwelling him at the stoning of Stephen left him after the entrance of light of revelation. No wonder God, through Paul, emphasised the need for revelations of the truth to the believer lest Christianity be mistaken for mere religious zealousness running from pillar to post but yet void of the attending darkness dispelling light of life.

Now to him that is of power to establish you according to my gospel, and the preaching of Jesus Christ, according to the revelation of the mystery, which was kept secret since the world began, But now is made manifest, and by the scriptures of the prophets, according to the commandment of the everlasting God, made known to all nations for the obedience of faith: To God only wise, be glory through Jesus Christ forever. Amen...Romans 6:25-27.

The scripture is the divine vault where truth is kept. The manifestation of this truth is hinged on revelation as seen in the above verses. The scriptures of the prophets and the commandments were available for years. The people had been reading and reciting them for years, but the real import was only made known to them when revelation came through Christ. Revelation is the only access to divine truth. Jesus speaking somewhere said it is given to the believers to know the mystery (hidden truth) of the kingdom (Luke 8:10). As the disciples were catching on in knowing this truth, Jesus' verdict was that they caught the truth because it was revealed.

At that time Jesus answered and said, I thank thee, O Father, Lord of heaven and earth, because thou hast hid these things from the wise and prudent, and hast revealed them unto babes. Even so, Father: for so it seemed good in thy sight. All things are delivered unto me of my Father: and no man knows the Son, but the Father; neither knows any man the Father, save the Son, and he to whomsoever the Son will reveal him.

Come unto me, all ye that labour and are heavy laden and I will give you rest. Take my yoke upon you, and learn of me; for I am meek and lowly in heart: and ye shall find rest unto your souls. For my yoke is easy, and my burden is light…Mathew 11:25-28.

Jesus was inviting humanity here unto freedom on the platform of revelation of the truth. The last three verses of the above scriptures are usually taken out of context as if Christ wants to do some magic. No wonder many feel frustrated after waiting for so long while nothing seems to change. But looking at the scripture closely, the whole conversation started in the context of Christ revealing the truth of and about God to whosoever positions him or herself in the learning place like a babe. The truth that can qualify for the belt today is still only accessible through revelation by Christ Jesus, but Christ is dead, risen, and gone to heaven, you might say. Yes and no I will answer.

And I will pray the Father, and He will give you

another Helper, that He may abide with you forever— the Spirit of truth, whom the world cannot receive, because it neither sees Him nor knows Him; but you know Him, for He dwells with you and will be in you. I will not leave you orphans; I will come to you...John 14:16-18.

The helper given to us by Jesus from the father is called the spirit of truth, which means his principal mission in our lives is to help us grasp the truth not just to speak with tongues. Jesus said when this comforter or Sprit of truth is in us, he Christ, is in us. To further help you see who and what the comforter is about, let us see what Christ said further.

But the Helper, the Holy Spirit, whom the Father will send in My name, He will teach you all things, and bring to your remembrance all things that I said to you...John14:26.

The helper is not another prophet or the last prophet as many liars will have us believe. He is the Holy Spirit whose principal mission is to teach us or reveal unto us the truth of redemption package. The helper Jesus referred to as coming after him was not Mohamed or any other prophet as you can see. The helper is the Holy Spirit of God.

Spirit Of Revelation

But as it is written: "Eye has not seen, nor ear heard, nor have entered into the heart of man the things which God has prepared for those who love Him.

But God has revealed them to us through His Spirit. For the Spirit searches all things, yes, the deep things of God. For what man knows the things of a man except the spirit of the man which is in him? Even so no one knows the things of God except the Spirit of God. Now we have received, not the spirit of the world, but the Spirit who is from God, that we might know the things that have been freely given to us by God. These things we also speak, not in words which man's wisdom teaches but which the Holy Spirit teaches, comparing spiritual things with spiritual. But the natural man does not receive the things of the Spirit of God, for they are foolishness to him; nor can he know them, because they are spiritually discerned...1 Corinthians 2:9-14.

No matter how smart and enlightened your mind is, you need the revelation of the truth through the help of the Holy Spirit before the mind of God, which is the fountain of truth, can be grasped. Every truth man will need for triumph has been given, and they are spiritual truths or realities. They are freely given as we can see but it takes the revelation of the Holy Spirit to know them and put them in the right perspective..."comparing spiritual things with spiritual." No wonder the Holy Spirit is referred to as the spirit of truth.

And I will pray the Father, and He will give you another Helper, that He may abide with you forever—the Spirit of truth, whom the world cannot receive, because it neither sees Him nor knows Him; but you know Him, for He dwells with you and will be in you...John14:16-17.

Three-Fold Cord

The Holy Spirit is at work in you as the Spirit of revelation. He is principally here to help you know the truth (knowledge). He will help you understand it so you put it in the right perspective (understanding). He will also help you appropriately apply it to the issue at hand in your life (wisdom).This forms the basis of the great prayer prayed for the Ephesians' believer by Paul the apostle.

Therefore I also, after I heard of your faith in the Lord Jesus and your love for all the saints, do not cease to give thanks for you, making mention of you in my prayers: that the God of our Lord Jesus Christ, the Father of glory, may give to you the spirit of wisdom and revelation in the knowledge of Him, the eyes of your understanding being enlightened; that you may know what is <u>the hope of His calling</u>, what are <u>the riches of the glory of His inheritance in the saints</u>, and what is <u>the exceeding greatness of His power toward us who</u>

believe, **according to the working of His mighty power which He worked in Christ when He raised Him from the dead and seated Him at His right hand in the heavenly places, far above all principality and power and might and dominion, and every name that is named, not only in this age but also in that which is to come.**

The simple descriptions of the three-fold cords that make up the belt of truth that guarantees your triumph in life's battle are:

(i) *The hope of your calling as a Christian.*

(ii) *The riches of God's glorious inheritance for you as a saint.*

(iii) *The greatness of God's power available unto you through Christ's resurrection.*

When these three-fold cords of the unbreakable belt of truth are in place, you cannot be stripped of victory by the enemy in whatever challenge of life, no matter how fierce they may be. This was the three-fold cord of the belt of truth that disarmed the devil when he came as bandit to strip Christ of his glorious destiny. Jesus knew the hope of his calling. He was sure of the riches of divine inheritance which he is the heir to. He also knew the availability of the exceeding great power of God toward him even before he was raised from the dead.

Let us see how the drama played out when Jesus Christ used his belt of truth to disarm the devil here on Earth.

Devil said to Christ-turn these stone to bread and eat.

Jesus said - no, I am not called just to eat bread as a man, am also called to eat word which is what I am doing in fasting; for man shall not live by bread alone but the hope of man's life is entrenched in every word that proceeds out of God's mouth. In other words, the word is enough to live by, there is no point manipulating stuff.

Devil said to Christ- bow down to me and I will make you rich and famous with enormous glory.

Jesus said - you dummy, can't you see I have a better inheritance full of glory and riches! As I worship and serve God alone, him being the owner of heavens and earth, line will soon be falling for me in pleasant places beyond what you can offer from what you stole.

Devil said to Christ -jump down and let's see if God is truly powerful enough to rescue you.

Jesus said – there is no point doing that, I know how exceedingly great the power God is, which he has made available for my rescue in time of trouble. I don't need to test it. People only test what they are not sure of and try what they have an iota of doubt may fail. But in this case, I have

no doubt as to my father's power to rescue. Watch out how he will demonstrate this great power by raising me up when you play your last card which is death.

The devil was too dull to understand what dimension of divine wisdom Christ was demonstrating, so he left him alone there and then. That was the day Christ sealed the destiny of hell and death concerning his death and resurrection, which would occur three and half years later. He knew fully and declared it to the devil that the rescuing power of God would later be available to him in the grave for resurrection when needed. There was, therefore, no point tempting or testing or trying it by jumping down hoping for a catch by angels. When the time came, he would willingly go to the slaughter with faith and not by trial and error. He knew divine power to rescue was not only real but available for his good in actualising his destiny and establishing him far above all principalities, might, power, and dominion. He also knew it would be made available when the need would arise at the appointed time. There was no point prompting the almighty. If Christ as a man had fallen by ignorance to the trap and jumped thereby testing God's power, he would have ended up an author and finisher of a faith based on trial and not on trust.

This same game is what the devil plays with people's minds when it comes to the miraculous healing today. You will hear folks mocking that if preachers are sure their God heals, they should come on a public stage where some disabled will be brought for the power the preachers are laying claim to be tested. Even in the days of Jesus and the Apostles, miraculous healings were not for the testers but "trusters" who believed in God's abilities to heal them. In peculiar cases, where such had no prior faith walk with God before, at the point of their healing, there was always that exhibition of belief in God's will or power to heal them and so they were healed. People have tempted God with their tithes and giving because they misunderstood a scripture, and when nothing changes in the outside, they go into the blame shell. I know it is all games and gimmick, they say. When confronted with the father of all lies, Jesus had his belt of truth on. The devil had no choice but to see that the battle of lies had been won by the belt of truth and leave Christ alone. Instead of Christ being stripped, it was the devil that was stripped. I pray this shall be your experience and testimonies from this day onward. Amen.

As great as this feat was, Jesus was only able to do it through the help of the Holy Spirit, which is also the Spirit of truth or revelation. Looking at the preceding verse, we clearly see who was in the driver sit at that material time.

Then Jesus, being filled with the Holy Spirit, returned from the Jordan and was led by the Spirit into the wilderness, being tempted for forty days by the devil. And in those days He ate nothing, and afterward, when they had ended, He was hungry. Luke 4:1-2.

It takes the Holy Spirit working in you as the spirit of wisdom and revelation in knowledge, not in ignorance and mere emotion, to open your eye of understanding to see in order to lay hold of and appropriately engage the truth as belt in conflicts of life. I will use a simple illustration of winning financial battle using the three-fold cord that constitutes the belt of truth to make you see how all of life's conflicts have a corresponding belt made available in the truth.

Hope Of Your Calling

Christianity is a call by God through the gospel of our Lord Jesus. Once you respond to it and become part of God's family. There is a hope or expectation set ahead of you. There is an eternal hope of living with God forever but there is also an arriving point or target set as expectation before you in all areas of life. If my present condition is contrary to this target, no matter what the facts are, it is still subject to change. The expression of this hope in the scripture is the only authentic final destination you can settle for as truth or reality.

For example, talking about money and finances, the scripture below clearly illustrates a picture of the hope of your financial calling:

For you know the grace of our Lord Jesus Christ, that though He was rich, yet for your sakes He became poor, that you through His poverty might become rich…2 Corinthians 8:9

The subject matter in this scripture was money, so rich, in this case, indicates having sufficient finances. The word "millionaire" or "billionaire" was not used here because they did not recon with such a word in the realm of the spirit, but there is something called "rich" there, which means having sufficiency in all things including finances. This is the hope or target of heaven for you. No matter how mitigating the lack and insufficiency on Earth is now, that is just a mere fact based on figures and experience. Once in Christ, the good fight of financial warfare starts when you start using the hope of your financial calling as part of the belt of truth to displace the facts of lack you are experiencing.

The same thing goes for all aspects of your life. There is a hope or target or expectation of heaven set ahead of you. No matter what the reality looks like now, the battle starts when you start imposing the eternal reality (truth) to displace the facts on ground.

When studying and fellowshipping with God's word, even the Bible, one of the principal tools constantly delivered into your hand is the hope of your calling as a believer, which cuts across all the various facets of your life.

For whatever things were written before were written for our learning, that we through the patience and comfort of the Scriptures might have hope...Romans 15:4

The Bible is therefore not just a moral book of rules and regulations as many would have us believe. It is even not just a book of promises. It is God's book of hope that sets before you your reality, even your expected end. If you will take the word of God as such, no matter where you are, it is only a matter of time until you get there.

My son, eat thou honey, because it is good; and the honeycomb, which is sweet to thy taste: So shall the knowledge of wisdom be unto thy soul: when thou hast found it, then there shall be a reward, and thy expectation shall not be cut off...Proverbs 24:13-14 (KJV).

The Riches Of God's Glorious Inheritance

God doesn't just give hope or set targets for us. He makes provisions for the journey there. God wanted us to be saints while we were sinners. He gave the blood of his son Jesus to cleanse us. Salvation was not just about the hope of a sinner becoming saint, but the provision of the means for the necessary conversion. For every hope of our calling, there is a wealth or riches of inheritance made available for us to get there by God. They are called inheritances and not just promise because they are already on ground and are made available as part of the family provisions.

As Christians, we are not just called to a hope, which is

the target. We are also called unto inheritances. Some of these inheritances came as promises in the Old Testament, but once Christ died and rose again, he obtained them for us as inheritances or family heritage accessible by new birth. Most Christians are still dwelling on promises when in reality God wants them to be seeing inheritances or provisions on ground. One of the greatest covenant accomplishments of Christ on our behalf is the conversion of promises to tangible inheritances for us.

For example, God promised to be a father to his people in the Old Testament on various occasions. But once Christ died and rose, it became a family inheritance for all who believe in him. Once faith believes in the present reality of a promise, it ceases to be just a promise but becomes an inheritance. Wherever you are going to in God, great and precious promises are made available to you as riches of inheritance. Making them your reality is an integral part of girding your loin with truth.

Talking about finances, one principal inheritance made available by God is for you to be guided into profiting by God himself. It is therefore not sufficient to know the hope of financial calling. It is also required to know the provision needed to get there. One example is seen below.

Thus says the LORD, your Redeemer, the Holy One of Israel: I am the LORD your God... who

teaches you to profit who leads you by the way you should go… Isaiah 48:17.

Part of the heritage or inheritances of believers that lead to wealth or profiting is to be led and guided into your large through your inner compass by God himself. When the enemy is trying to get you stuck in a dry place of life, your inheritance is to be led out of such dry place into a wealthy place. This does not necessarily mean a geographical change of location. It could be same place, same job, same business but in another way. Your awareness of this reality (truth) will change your attitude, prayer, and attention at such a time. You will see God's dead commitment to guide and lead you out of such a dry place. You will also be ready to be led, putting premium on divine signals within than the dryness around you.

The Exceeding Greatness Of His Power Toward Us Who Believe

No matter how glorious the hope of God's calling for you is, no matter how rich and precious the inheritance of the saints are, it takes empowerment for things to work in God's kingdom.

For the kingdom of God is not in word but in power…1 Corinthians 4:20

Even though the hope of God's calling for Jesus was for him to be a saviour through death and resurrection, and part of the riches of his inheritance was a name above all names, it still took the power of God through the spirit of holiness for that eternal reality to be delivered here on Earth.

Paul, a bondservant of Jesus Christ, called to be an apostle, separated to the gospel of God which He promised before through His prophets in the Holy Scriptures, concerning His Son Jesus Christ our Lord, who was born of the seed of David according to the flesh, and declared to be the Son of God with power according to the Spirit of holiness, by the resurrection from the dead...Romans 1:1-4.

The reality or truth is that God's empowerment is always available to establish the reality or truth in your life. This is well captured below:

Blessed be the God and Father of our Lord Jesus Christ, who according to His abundant mercy has begotten us again to a living hope through the resurrection of Jesus Christ from the dead, to an inheritance incorruptible and undefiled and that does not fade away, reserved in heaven for you, who are kept by the power of God through faith for salvation ready to be revealed in the last time.1 Peter 1:3-5

For example, in financial matters, blessing is an empowerment not a material thing. But this same empowerment eventually makes us rich if channelled into our finances.

The blessing of the LORD makes one rich, and He adds no sorrow with it…Proverbs 10:22

God's expectation or hope for you is to be materially sufficient, which is part of the hope of your calling. He therefore made available for you precious inheritances as promised in the word. But the belt of truth concerning finances is not yet in place until the issue of empowerment to prosper is in place. This empowerment to prosper is part of the ministry of the Holy Spirit on your life, even the same spirit of power that raised Christ from the dead.

Spiritual warfare is not about rolling up the sleeves of your shirt or screaming. The battles of life are too sophisticated for that, and there are spiritual techniques to employ through the word of God, lest you start punching the air generating nothing whatsoever in impact.

There is no cease fire in this war front. Once enrolled, you are in the battle for ever, which is why you cannot be fighting as punching the air lest you become exasperated, give up, and lose out.

The belt of truth is for your loin, and your loin is your mind. The battle-ground of life is principally your mind, until the mind is tacked and bound up with the eternal reality (truth) on the issue on ground; all other efforts are waste of time and armour.

Therefore gird up the loins of your mind, be sober, and rest your hope fully upon the grace that is to be brought to you at the revelation of Jesus Christ…1 Peter 1:13.

Starting with the belt of truth was not a mistake but a deliberate inspiration by God while the scripture was being given. Until the mind battle is won, spiritual warfare is a futile exercise. I have people say that all battles are fought in the mind. Not really, the Bible never says so. As we look at our anchor scripture further, we shall see that the armour is not worn on the same part of the body throughout. The only one for the loin (mind) is the belt of truth. Funny enough, no one starts dressing by putting the belt on first. But in spiritual warfare, the first element to put on is the belt of truth meant for the loin of your mind. Sure, you are not asked to put the shield of faith on your loin or the shoe of the gospel on your loin, not even prayer. What garrisons man's mind against the onslaught of the adversary is the belt of truth. The mind is not the battle ground for all life's battles, but the mind is the first battle ground of all life's' battles. The battle of truth is fought and won in the mind; this is the starting point for all that will end up well in spiritual warfare.

I have seen people exercising great faith on issues and doing everything seemingly right and yet are at the verge of giving up because the belt of truth is slack. The eternal reality of their position is not girding their minds or all together absent concerning the issue at hand. Truly they are in faith, but while faith procures the break through from on high, it takes staying through for the breakthrough to manifest in the earthly realm. Thus, you are admonished to add patience to your faith. What many call patience is just waiting for the result they feel they have not received, but patience is waiting on the result you have received by faith till it manifests. When you understand this, time makes no difference in your reckoning again, but when you don't, the enemy will start bombarding your mind with questions to bring in confusion and eventually weaken the faith you had earlier. The cycle can continue till only God knows, but understanding, which is an integral part of revelation, is what will make available unto you the belt with which to gird the loin of your mind against the onslaught of the devil at such a time. The most pain folks feel when waiting upon God for something they have not gotten is not the pain of not having that thing (they probably have been living without it before anyway) but the pain of unanswered questions of why and what. Some will even start asking if something is wrong with them or with God. If care is not taken, discouragement will set in and apathy of a kind toward the thing of the spirit. You need to know you are in a fight, not necessarily against a demon but a fight against the seen reality or facts. It takes you holding on to the revelation of unseen facts or realities and girding your mind with the same to stay through for your breakthrough.

The good fight of faith starts with the loin guarded with

truth. The mind is the gate-way to the spirit. It is also the gate-way to the body. The belt of truth is the only true guard that can safeguard your spirit, soul, and body in the conflicts of life. Once in place, no matter your present struggle or condition, the peace of God will keep you for your trophies. Most agitations and worries in the battle fronts of life are an indication of the loin not yet guarded or garrisoned enough with the truth. Just lie Christ said that he stands at the door (mind) knocking, victory is knocking from on high, defeat and despair are knocking from hell. The belt of truth is the true and faithful guard to employ as gate keeper of your mind. Once in place, it does not open the door for defeat and despair, it will only allow the peace of God that passes all understanding or common sense and reasoning to garrison or fence your mind from the heat and the hurts of battles. This is what it takes to fight and win in peace and style as if no war is actually going on.

Knowledge And Truth

Jesus was not rabble rousing. He was not out to make an intellectual or oratorical point. He was out to win a battle, so he went straight to the point, engaging the right tool for the conflict and rested his case. Jesus was not quoting the scripture and running helter skelter at the same time. He was not quoting with his mouth and doing the opposite with his legs like quoting and turning the stone to bread fearing he may die of hunger if he did not do so. His actions indeed betrayed what he knew and what was in him was found to eventually be the truth.

Knowing and quoting the truth is never equal to the belt of truth but taking a stand in your words, body language and actions. Every educated person can read or hear the word and have a literal knowledge of what is being said. The knowledge of truth is only validated by what you say and do. As long as the children of Israel were busy crying and throwing tantrums in the wilderness for the temporary inconveniences that was meant to last for 40 days, God said they did not know the truth about man and bread. It took them 40 years to eventually learn and know it. That was when they got promoted out of that phase of life!

Every commandment which I command you today you must be careful to observe, that you may live and multiply, and go in and possess the land of which the LORD swore to your fathers. And you shall remember that the LORD your God led you all the way these forty years in the wilderness, to humble you and test you, to know what was in your heart, whether you would keep His commandments or not. So He humbled you, allowed you to hunger, and fed you with manna which you did not know nor did your fathers know, <u>that He might make</u> you know that man shall not live by bread alone; but man lives by every word that proceeds from the mouth of the Lord...Deuteronomy 8:1-3.

God said, the wilderness was only necessary because of the need for the people to know an essential truth they did not know at the onset of the journey. This shows that if they had known it, it would have shown in their words, attitudes, and actions when the war of hunger and thirst broke out. When the going was rough, God did not pretend or deny the fact that it was rough. But God said that in spite of the challenges there would not have been any need for the long journey. Forty days would have been 40 days and not 40 years.

We live in the age of knowledge, (Daniel 12:4), but what matters is the knowledge of truth. This goes beyond mental information but a consciousness and awareness of the truth, which shows and reflects in your actions and reactions in the face of challenges. To know the truth is making it part and parcel of your consciousness and awareness. You are not acting in order to prove any religious or doctrinal point. You are just living out your awareness. It does not matter how ugly the situation is. With your belt in place, you are holding firm to the end unmoved from the liberty which Christ bought for you with his precious life.

Life On Earth; A Conflict Of Realities

You are in a battle that can be simply referred to as conflict of realities, the eternal reality in God versus the temporal reality of facts, truth settled in heaven versus facts settled on earth.

If care is not taken, because of the persistence of and the perspiration brought about by life's conflicts and challenges, one can easily fall into the trap of seeing the on pass of life as the unchangeable reality of destiny in God. It is pretty comforting for the flesh to accept the facts on ground as the ultimate reality even when the word of God says it is subject to change. It is easier and requires no effort to settle for "fate" than to walk in faith. *Newton's first law of motion rightly says that inertia or comfort zone of rest is a cheaper alternative except one is ready to make the effort of applying a compelling force to effect the desired change.* The mitigating circumstances you are facing are tenaciously, holding on to the facts on ground, they are also deceptive, looking unchangeable. The father of wiles is making the facts look like they are deep-seated and eternal and unmovable, but the word of truth would have you know that the facts on ground are subject to displacement.

That is why we never give up. Though our bodies are dying, our spirits are being renewed every day. For our present troubles are small and won't last very long. Yet they produce for us a glory that vastly outweighs them and will last forever! So we don't look at the troubles we can see now; rather, we fix our gaze on things that cannot be seen. For the things we see now will soon be gone, but the things we cannot see will last forever…2 Corinthians 4:16-18 (NLV)

In the conflict of realities, you are admonished not to give up. The pain may be so hurtful, past efforts met with frustration, and nothing seems more real than the bad situation on ground. Don't ever give up. You are in the battle of realities. The truth, that is the eternal reality in God, should be the hold round the loin of your mind to help you fix your gaze. The facts will soon be gone, your eternal reality in heavenly places shall find full fledge expression for ever in earthly places soon.

Yinka Akintunde

CHAPTER 03

THE BODY ARMOUR

Stand your ground, putting on the belt of truth and the body armour of God's righteousness...Ephesians 6:14 (NLT).

The breast plate of righteousness is particularly well-rendered as body armour of righteousness in this translation of the Bible. It is the essential part of the armour worn like a suit to cover your body and, in particular, your chest where your heart, the seat of your conscience, is. The breastplate or body armour is to protect you from all the offensives launched in particular against your heart to destroy your conscience. The question you may ask is, how important is my conscience in the battle of life?

I will say very important. Life battle for a believer is essentially described as a fight of faith.

Fight the good fight of faith, lay hold on eternal life, whereunto thou art also called, and hast professed a good profession before many witnesses…1Timothy 6:12.

Having seen many challenges and fought many battles, Paul the Apostle summarized all the fights he fought as just one fight and one that hinged on keeping the faith for that matter.

I have fought a good fight, I have finished my course, I have kept the faith…2 Timothy 4:7a

When the devil went all out for Peter in life's battle at the point of master's death, Jesus described the battle as a battle of faith as well.

And the Lord said, "Simon, Simon! Indeed, Satan has asked for you, that he may sift you as wheat. But I have prayed for you, that your faith should not fail; and when you have returned to me, strengthen your brethren …Luke 22:31-32.

In fighting the battles of life, which are essentially battles of faith, a good conscience determines whether the warship stays afloat or sinks. Going down or sinking in the waters of challenges is not just about being a believer or a person of faith, but having a good conscience toward God and man.

This charge I commit to you, son Timothy, according to the prophecies previously made concerning you, that by them you may wage the good warfare, having faith and a good conscience, which some having rejected, concerning the faith have suffered shipwreck …1Timothy 1:18-19.

The warfare is as good as the conscience is, simply put. Many of us think that mere faith is all it takes and so we have these proliferation of modern-day self belief, which is void of God's consciousness leaving many lives and destinies sinking unnecessarily in its trail.

IMPUTED

When we talk of a good conscience, it is based on the righteousness imputed to you through forgiveness of sin and that which is imparted in you as one who is born of God. At salvation, the blood of Jesus cleans you of all sins and the evil or guilty conscience that goes with it thereby giving you the right standing with and before God. At this point, God sees you as a guiltless saint who is at peace or in one with him every wit.

But now the righteousness of God apart from the law is revealed, being witnessed by the Law and the Prophets, even the righteousness of God, through faith in Jesus Christ, to all and on all who believe. For there is no difference; for all have sinned and fall short of the glory of God, being justified freely by His grace through the

redemption that is in Christ Jesus…Romans 3: 21-24.

When you are born again, you are not going to gradually attain righteousness. You have attained it by the finished work of Christ. Righteousness does not come by fasting, vowing, celibacy, or giving alms. All these could be good works with their respective rewards when done in true fear and service of the Lord, but they do not equate or make anyone righteous. Righteousness is a gift from God through Christ Jesus. It has got nothing to do with your person. It is a gift from God.

For if by one man's offence death reigned by one; much more they which receive abundance of grace and of the gift of righteousness shall reign in life by one, Jesus Christ…Romans5:17

You do not feel righteous, just like humans do not need to feel human to know they are human. You just know you are human by consciousness borne out of awareness. The New Testament attitude to righteousness is a knowing attitude, not a feeling attitude. The righteousness of believers is the very nature of God imputed and imparted unto human, but I have heard Christians say things like having the filthy rag kind of righteousness and quoting Isaiah 64:6. What a miss! People say so because their knowledge of righteousness is of self righteousness and not the God righteousness imputed to them at salvation. This is what it means to go about establishing your own and rejecting God's own righteousness. If your Christian' righteousness is like a filthy rag, so is God's righteousness, and God forbid that the holy and righteous God be filthy. Christian' righteousness is God's righteousness given to you by faith in the Son of God. The difference between the filthy rag kind of righteousness and the God-imputed righteousness is shown below. (The word rubbish is rendered as dung or flit, just like filthy rag in the old King James Version of the Bible.)

But what things were gain to me, these I have counted loss for Christ. Yet indeed I also count all things loss for the excellence of the knowledge of Christ Jesus my Lord, for whom I have suffered the loss of all things, and <u>count them as rubbish</u>, that I may gain Christ and be found in Him, not having my own righteousness, which is from the law, but that which is through faith in Christ, the righteousness which is from God by faith... Philippians 3:7-9.

IMPARTED

Righteousness is not a title. It is a status imputed to us or our account by God so we can have a right stand with and before him, but there is more to it. With your new birth, righteousness being God's nature is also imparted to you as the divine ability to live right before God and please him. This is so crucial because as we saw earlier that in life's battle you are not on your own but in partnership with God, and the partnership only works when you and he are in agreement. Your ability or readiness to punish any disobedience from hell is hinged on your obedience to God, too. **2 Corinthians 10:6.**

God will not leave you in an incapacitated or vulnerable state in life's battle. That is why you are not just given a free deposit of righteousness (imputing) but you are also given the ability to live right by God's standard (imparting). God's nature and ability are thereby working in you both to will and do of his good pleasure.

Therefore, my beloved, as you have always obeyed, not as in my presence only, but now much more in my absence, work out your own salvation with fear and trembling; for it is God who works in you both to will and to do for His good pleasure…Philippians…2:13-14

Imparted righteousness makes you to always want to do it right before God all the time. That is why you do not feel comfortable in error or sin if you fall into one, seeing it is contrary to your nature, now that you are born of God. You do not just do right when people are there or that you may be commended of religious folks. You do right because that is the only way compatible with your nature. No one can please God through human or fleshly effort even after being saved. God's grace or ability is given to you to live right and be comfortable within only when you do. You are doing right because you have been imbibed with the ability to do so by God.

Little children, let no one deceive you. He who practices righteousness is righteous, just as He is righteous...1 John 3:7.

When a man starts barking like a dog or bleating like a sheep while communicating, we know something is wrong somewhere. In order to be heard properly he will have to switch back to human language if he is to be taken serious in any conversation at all. If you find yourself in sin, thereby doing unrighteousness, which is contrary to your nature by new birth. It is part of your nature and is expected of you to make a turn by repentance and come back to your true self, doing that which is right.

Righteousness puts you on vantage platforms as you pitch your battle against the enemy. These platforms we shall see below.

(i) **Boldness**

> **The wicked flee when no one pursues, but the righteous are bold as a lion...Proverbs 28:1**

This lion, we are told, is a strong animal that turns not away in battle. The offensive audacity with which it lays claim on its prey is such that puts the prey in no other position but to flee or be destroyed. God does not want you to run from pillar to post chased by cockroaches, rats, men, and the devil. To be audacious as a lion, you need to walk in righteousness, and if you sin there is no explanation that justifies sin rather than to confess it to the Lord, get cleansed, and move away from the compromised position. In Christianity, bold face does not win but rather a pure boldness rooted in your oneness with God, which is enhanced by righteousness as written above. You do not have to carry sin consciousness around like a garment, looking for fault and sin in everything and everyone. Living in guilt will drain your energy and leave you defenceless. Praying Psalm 50 in all meetings as sign of humility is a reflection of lack of understanding. David prayed that because he sinned and he knew he sinned. It was not an everyday prayer for him. You do not have to keep begging for forgiveness of sins every time in order to look humble before God. A Christian does not practice sin. That is why it is called being overtaken with a fault or caught in sin in the Bible - Galatians 6:1. The enemy you are principally fighting is called the accuser, and he is ready to compromise your boldness through guilt. In order to fight him to a standstill, you need a purged conscience.

(ii)   **Divine Presence**

> **But to the Son He says: your throne, O God, is forever and ever; a sceptre of righteousness is the sceptre of your kingdom. You have loved righteousness and hated lawlessness; therefore God, Your God, has anointed you with the oil of gladness more than your companions...Hebrews 1:8-9**

No matter how skilful you are, the armour of God delivers because God is present. As soon as you become saved, the first thing God does is to tabernacle in you. This underscores the importance of divine presence. The fact that God is present somewhere does not mean that God is allowed to act freely there. God is omnipresent but it is obvious he is not actively involved everywhere. The anointing is the active involvement or the abiding presence of God in the affairs of men. Christ's triumph in life as a man was a working of the divine presence resident in and on him.

> **And he that sent me is with me: the Father hath not left me alone; for I do always those things that please him...John 8:29.**

This was the emphatic declaration of Christ when the battle was fierce. At this point, all kinds of opposition were being orchestrated from hell against his destiny through the scribes and other religious and non-religious folks of his days, yet he was the winner at the end of the battle orchestrated by the devil. He won because divine presence was evidently solid round about him.

Let's see two other scriptures to appreciate the import of divine presence in the conflict of life.

When Israel went out of Egypt, The house of Jacob from a people of strange language, Judah became His sanctuary, And Israel His dominion. The sea saw it and fled; Jordan turned back. The mountains skipped like rams, the little hills like lambs. What ails you, O sea that you fled? O Jordan that you turned back? O mountains that you skipped like rams? O little hills, like lambs? Tremble, O earth, at the presence of the Lord, at the presence of the God of Jacob...Psalm 114:1-7

The mountains and hills represent challenges, the seas and Jordan being hindrances to forward movement and forces that are ready to sweep you off your feet. Yet they all fled when divine presence did manifest on the scene. The forces of darkness will not come and fight you as a demon with horns and ugly face, but will rather make life's situations so ugly and unbearable, throwing all kinds of hindrances and challenges on your path in order for you to give in and give up. The breastplate of righteousness guarantees divine presence in a profound way that guarantees your winning no matter how deep the sea or high the mountain you are facing now may be.

As the mountains surround Jerusalem, so the LORD surrounds His people from this time forth and forever…Psalms125:2

When divine presence is manifest in your conflict, God's presence is not just there to rescue you but much more to shield you from the onslaught. You therefore won't live in fear looking back over your shoulder all the time in panic. You are not praying to be protected. You are conscious of your divine protection. In fact, the scripture says at this realm the wicked has no capacity or ability to touch you.

We know that whoever is born of God does not sin; but he who has been born of God keeps himself, and the wicked one does not touch him…1John 5:18.

(iii)   Foundation For The Winning Heritage

Let the saints be joyful in glory: let them sing aloud upon their beds. Let the high praises of God be in their mouth, and a two-edged sword in their hand; To execute

vengeance upon the heathen, and punishments upon the people; To bind their kings with chains, and their nobles with fetters of iron; To execute upon them the judgment written: these honours have all his saints. Praise ye the LORD…Psalms 149:5-9.(KJV).

The saints here are not the canonized ones, but the ones who have been made righteous in God and are living it out. The canonized ones cannot praise God nor fight any battle again as the Bible says that the dead cannot praise God (Psalms 115:17). The saints here are, therefore, the ones who have been made righteous in and by God. To take two-edged sword in their hand shows that the other weapons in the armoury will maximally and easily deliver when the sainthood of the saint is not compromised.

No weapon formed against you shall prosper, and every tongue which rises against you in judgment you shall condemn. This is the heritage of the servants of the LORD, and their righteousness is from me, says the LORD…Isaiah 54:17

God is saying that as long as the gift of righteousness he gave you is kept intact, nothing is strong enough to destroy you no matter who fabricates it.

God's inclusion of the breastplate of righteousness in the armour is not to trap you into defeat but to set you up for victory, which is why he imputed you with his own righteous nature and imparted you with the abilities necessary to live it out here on Earth.

In warfare, identity is very important. Who you are matters more than how skilful you are, because the level of armoury made available to you or set against you is a function of which side of the battle line you belong. Thank God you are on God's side. There is no greater force in heaven, hell, or earth than the arsenal of heaven.

Finally, I need to say here that as sickness weakens the physical body so does sin to the human spirit. Just as sicknesses leads to death if untreated so sin does to the spirit if not repented of. Just as a sick person cannot go to battle front because of the compromise in his body functioning and performance, so will sin compromise the effectiveness of your spirit man in life's battle if untreated, no matter how skilful or well-trained you are in the art of warfare.
You are in the righteous camp of God. You are given the righteousness of God as a breastplate or body armour. My prayer is that you keep it on so that no fiery dart of the wicked can penetrate you.

Yinka Akintunde

CHAPTER 04

GOOD NEWS, GOOD STEPS

And having shod your feet with the preparation of the gospel of peace...Ephesians 6:15 (KJV)

The readiness that comes through the Gospel is what the New International Version (NIV) calls the "preparation of the Gospel," and it really captures the subject at hand perfectly. I know a lot of us know that we need to share the Gospel of salvation through our Lord Jesus with everybody on earth. Yes, it is our calling and a duty we must attend to with all diligence. But then this particular verse of the scripture in context of the whole passage goes beyond preaching the gospel to the unsaved. The truth is that a gospel you are not consciously walking in cannot be effectively communicated by you to anybody. The gospel goes beyond words. It is an experience.

For I am not ashamed of the gospel of Christ, for it is the power of God to salvation for everyone who believes, for the Jew first and also for the Greek…Romans1:16

The truth is you do not preach power, you experience it! The sure thing about power is its ability to exert or effect change. When we talk about the gospel or good news we are talking of the divine ability made available unto you to effect good changes in your life as you journey through.

Having walked on slippery unpaved roads before, experience shows that the rapid mud is not just out to befall you but to slip whatever footwear you are putting on away from your feet if not well fastened. This is the background for the military term used in this reference verse for this chapter. To "shod" your feet is not the same thing as to just put something on, rather to fasten it tight on your feet as someone going into a slippery terrain for military expeditions. You are not just expected to flippantly and carelessly walk in the good news. You are expected to violently fasten it to your feet knowing fully that there are many rapid slippery muds out there wanting to remove the good from your news and knock you off your path of victory and destiny.

In as much as Christ has already finished the legal deal of the New Testament or covenant on your behalf, testament needs enforcement after the death of the testator especially if there are opposing parties still roaming around to contend with.

For where a testament is, there must also of necessity be the death of the testator. For a testament is of force after men are dead: otherwise it is of no strength at all while the testator lives…Hebrews 9:16-17

The strength of a will is in its enforcement. The Gospel news is good. The content of the testament is better, but the reality of its experience is only guaranteed in your life when you personally enforce it or forcefully walk in it consciously. The readiness or preparation of the Gospel is therefore your conscious walking in the good news the Lord Jesus Christ brought to mankind, making it an experience, allowing it to affect all facets of your life. This is the effective way of establishing God's kingdom on earth. For a lot of folks, good news finishes after they are born again. Speeches like "walking with God is not easy", "expect and accept calamities" become their holy slogan. If walking with the good God means pain, struggles, tears, and sorrow as many will have us believe, I wonder what walking on the other side of the road with the wicked devil will be. What good there is in the good news then if it is all about pain, sorrow, and failure. I am not in the denial of everyday challenges, which are universal and inevitable to everyone, but there is good news made available as shoes that you are expected to put on to buffer and secure your steps in victory and bring the ease of triumph into your path. A Christian is not helpless in the face of challenges. You are not left by the good God without the good solution to the entire bad problem in a dark world.

Jesus said the Gospel yoke is an easy yoke – Matthew 12:18. The Bible here calls it the Gospel of peace. It brings peace into the warring parts of your life. Most Christians think the Gospel or the good news is for unbelievers alone, what an error. The Gospel offers only one thing to an unbeliever and that is salvation of their soul from the eternal doom of sin. But the Gospel has more in stock than the salvation from sin. In fact, the Gospel of Christ is more relevant to the saints than the sinner. If it was not so, God would not ask you to still put it on as armour after salvation.

For the message of the cross is foolishness to those who are perishing, but to us who are being saved it is the power of God For it is written: I will destroy the wisdom of the wise, And bring to nothing the understanding of the prudent. Where is the wise? Where is the scribe? Where is the disputer of this age? Has not God made foolish the wisdom of this world? For since, in the wisdom of God, the world through wisdom did not know God, it pleased God through the foolishness of the message preached to save those who believe. For Jews request a sign, and Greeks seek after wisdom; but we preach Christ crucified, to the Jews a stumbling block and to the Greeks foolishness, but to those who are called, both Jews and Greeks, Christ the power of God and the wisdom of God…1Corinthians 1:18-24.

I hear people preach everything to saints in church except the good news, all kinds of evil reports of how it is so difficult to please God or live happily as a Christian, how it is impossible to get it right in life and still go to heaven. Bad news all the way is what they deliver. Many feel the good news is just to lead people to the gate of Zion, a kind of enticement or bait to get you into the church, but once you are in, the good news ends. They will have us believe that once the good news takes care of the sin problem, you are just left on your own in the cold hand of struggles while the good news goes back outside looking for another victim to entice. But the very good God does not run His kingdom that way. The good news belongs in here. It belongs in Zion. Good news is an in-house menu much more than it is an invitational call for the outsiders. Christianity is good news all the way, Jesus at the beginning of His ministry, which was the very end of the old covenant and the dawn of the new covenant, in which we are called Christian, made a profound statement:

The Spirit of the LORD is upon Me, because He has anointed Me to preach the gospel to the poor; He has sent Me to heal the broken hearted, to proclaim liberty to the captives and recovery of sight to the blind, to set at liberty those who are oppressed…Luke 4:18.

Everything above is good. Nothing short of good is in the gospel according to Christ, and he also said the fulfilment of the good in the news is now, not when we are dead and gone to heaven only.

Zion Menu For Today

And He began to say to them, "Today this Scripture is fulfilled in your hearing...Luke 4:21.

Christ was also saying here that as profound and promising as the statements were, they were not just a mere philosophical saying or enticing word of eloquence, but rather the gospel is **"a scripture"** that is given by God "for an appointed time" which is expected to be fulfilled in you as you hear it. Jesus was saying here that the gospel is a particular scripture set for a particular time.
What scripture?

The Spirit of the Lord GOD is upon me, because the LORD has anointed me to preach good tidings to the poor; He has sent me to heal the broken hearted, to proclaim liberty to the captives, and the opening of the prison to those who are bound... Isaih61:1

The scripture Christ referred to as being fulfilled as the gospel is seen above. It was a scripture given in the old covenant but set for fulfilment in the new one we are in now. If the particular scripture had started and ended there, we might as well have concluded that the gospel is probably meant majorly for the outsiders, but there is more to the menu package in the gospel than this first verse. So let's see the whole picture of what the gospel is.

To proclaim the acceptable year of the LORD, and the day of vengeance of our God; to comfort all who mourn, to console those who mourn in Zion, to give them beauty for ashes, The oil of joy for mourning, The garment of praise for the spirit of heaviness; That they may be called trees of righteousness, the planting of the LORD, that He may be glorified...Isaiah 61:2-3.

Appointed To Be Given

The bulk of what the gospel carries is meant to be distributed and consumed within Zion as we can see, and Zion is the Church where believers dwell.

But you have come to Mount Zion and to the city of the living God, the heavenly Jerusalem, to an innumerable company of angels, to the general assembly and church of the firstborn who are registered in heaven, to God the Judge of all, to the spirits of just men made perfect, to Jesus the Mediator of the new covenant, and to the blood of sprinkling that speaks better things than that of Abel. Hebrews 12:22-24

Zion is not referring to the sinners' world out there. Zion is the spiritual home base for all saints where God is referred to as father and Christ Jesus the mediator of the covenant of better deals contained in the good news. Zion is where divine comfort ought to replace mourning. When life's journey becomes so painful and all you can naturally do is to mourn and play the blame game, put on the shoes of good news and be comforted. For every pain the enemy wants to inflict so that you may keep mourning, there is a comfort in Zion you can lay hold of, to turn the table in your favour.

The old King James Version renders the word console as "to appoint to them that mourn in Zion." For every issue causing mourning, there is a gospel entity appointed by God to terminate the mourning, it is your duty to search out the appointment letter written for you in the scripture and lay hold of the hope of the gospel or good news in it. This becomes the anchor for your drifting soul. Then you can wipe your face, stop the worrying, and start declaring your appointment, releasing all the forces of heaven ordained for your comfort till you see the situation changed for your good.

For whatever things were written before were written for our learning, that we through the patience and comfort of the Scriptures might have hope…Romans15:4

The scripture is given to us according to 2 Timothy 3:16 so that you can search out your own appointed lot and appointment letters, which you are expected to present in the ware-house of life every time so that, that which had been procured by Christ on your behalf might be given to you every time they are needed. There is nothing Christ did not pay for on your behalf in things that pertain to life and godliness.

...but we preach Christ crucified, to the Jews a stumbling block and to the Greeks foolishness, but to those who are called, both Jews and Greeks, Christ the power of God and the wisdom of God...1Corinthians1:18-24.

Every package of the gospel is made available unto you in the gospel either as power, which is divine ability within your spirit to leap over wall and pass through troupes. It could also be made available as wisdom to your heart, which is the sure and God's way of approach to issue. This gospel package of power and wisdom guarantee your victory and joy no matter how knotty or bad the case may be.

Let me help you further. Verses two and three of Isaiah 61 talk of you being given beauty whenever the wicked throws ashes at you. You are also given the oil of joy to wipe off the heat and friction of mourning. The gospel is to strip you of the garment of heaviness, which can lead to suicide, depression, and low self-esteem. The good news is to put upon you the merry that makes for praise that culminates in a change of standing and position which eventually glorifies God. Zion is the place of being given, where the oil flows, where mourning stops, where praise is like a garment on your spirit. The good news is relevant to you in Zion, much more than when you were outside.

The sad reality in life is many are waiting for their appointment letter in Zion, whereas God is waiting on them to appoint unto themselves the letter already written and dispatched on their behalf. But aren't the anointed ones specially assigned to appoint those good portions to everyone in Zion, you ask. Yes, the anointed ones are the appointed ones sent to give beauty for ashes in Zion. I see, that is why I have been waiting for my appointment with my anointed so things can change. Maybe my file is at the bottom in heaven. My turn may come sooner or later, you say. No, you are missing the point. You are the first anointed one sent to you for your own appointments in the kingdom! Once you have the spirit of God in you, you are anointed for your appointment in life. This is one of the reasons why God makes a priest and king (royal priesthood) (anointed ones) out of you primarily once you are saved.

But you have an anointing from the Holy One, and you know all things.... But the anointing which you have received from Him abides in you, and you do not need that anyone teach you; but as the same anointing teaches you concerning all things, and is true, and is not a lie, and just as it has taught you, you will abide in Him...1 John 2:20 &27.

You are the anointed one!

You are first sent to you, which is what the scripture is emphasising with verse 27. The Bible is not saying you should not be taught by your spiritual leaders because you are anointed, but that you are empowered by the divine presence in you to appoint unto yourself your beauty for ashes, the oil of joy for mourning, and garment of praise for the spirit of heaviness. Stop waiting for someone to come and do it for you. We are in a "DIY" kingdom! Do it yourself, through Christ or the anointing who strengthens you.

Search out your appointment letters from the word of God and appoint or appropriate them accordingly. You probably do not like what your background has appointed unto you. No need crying. Tear up the evil appointments and search out the one apportioned to you by your heavenly father. Your spiritual background preceded and supersedes your natural background. Thus God told Jeremiah that before he entered a natural background through his mother's womb; he God had appointed good things, with which to pull down evil and establish good, for him in his spiritual background (Jeremiah 1:4-5).

The word of God is packaged with all that you need to stop mourning. The good news is to appoint unto you your own portion of the good in Zion. Appoint unto to you your spouse, appoint unto you your stuffs. All you need is to get the appointment letter and hold on to it tenaciously. Instead of mourning, seek out what has been appointed to you. There are many beautifying stuffs that have been given to you as heritage in Christ. No wonder we are told we met some inheritances in Zion and were given all things that make life comfortable eventually no matter the hardship you met on ground.

Blessed be the God and Father of our Lord Jesus Christ, who according to His abundant mercy has begotten us again to a living hope through the resurrection of Jesus Christ from the dead, to an inheritance incorruptible and undefiled and that does not fade away, reserved in heaven for you...1 Peter1:3.

Jesus said, come to me and I will give you rest. Our God is a giving God. He gives liberally as well. Search out what you have been given. In Zion there is the oil of joy to lubricate your life engine or else you will be worn out under pressure and challenges of life. Many saints are worn out and make God to look like a prayer storing, offering eating task master, and it ought not to be so!

I remember a clothes dealer approaching one of the sisters known to me way back trying to advertise her wares. She said, "Sister, I have a lot of beautiful dresses to sell and Christian dresses as well." When the sister told me, I was grieved within, because what she meant by Christian dress were some second-hand, non-fitting dresses worn probably when cotton wool was just discovered! The cloth seller, a believer also, said so proudly because that was the paradigm of low life taken for Christianity. She was made to believe that second-hand clothes, which invariably were cheap probably and worn while new by an unbeliever, now belong to saints as a show of piety, humility and moderation. What an assault and insult on redemption price. But I did not blame her much. She was taught that Christians are the never-happy, never-do-well; always-frowning Jones next door who are going to heaven and are not even excited about it and so are ever sad waiting for their flight. But that is the lie of the devil against Zion. Out of Zion the perfection of beauty God hath shined. **Psalm 50:2.**

God brought you to Zion, by the gospel which is the good news. By the same gospel or good news he will beautify you. Stop your mourning. Unburden your spirit so that men seeing you will know that you are planted by God to outlast all storms thereby glorifying him. When you walk in the consciousness of this good news, the power of God is made available unto your spirit for performance and wisdom comes your way showing you what to do.

Your feet being shod or fitted with the good news is a deliberate thing, just like you do not stumble into any shoe while dressing up or just find yourself in any shoe while going for outing. So are you to consciously and deliberately fit your feet in what you want to walk in and walk in it. It is time to seek out the right shoe for the right occasion, the healing shoe as the good news for your healing against sicknesses and diseases, the character shoe for the kind of marriage you so desire, prosperity shoe for your financial needs. Soundness of mind, boldness, worry free, and all good things of life have their shoes made available in the good news package. Keep getting yours to walk in. When you are just sitting down mourning and waiting for things to happen somehow by themselves, it is like going out barefooted hoping that a pair of good shoes will just jump on your feet one way or the other. Quit such fantasy, God is not a magician. All he has done is to make available for you the good news through his word. It is your duty to find it, work it, and thus walk it as shoes. You only enjoy the shoe when you walk in it. It is of no use on the shelf. The only things that happen by themselves are mostly bad things or nothing at all. Good things are made to happen in life by someone.

You are appointed and anointed by God to make good things happen to you first and then to others. When you consciously search out the covenants of the gospel and deliberately position yourself to walk in their realities, you are already fighting a good warfare. When the enemy brings on the bad news and you chose to stay in the good news, it is a matter of time before your victory will be out for all to see.

The good news of God through Christ Jesus is a weapon of warfare, which gives you power to fight and wisdom to win.

Good news are not flattering sweet talks, they are divine provisions in Zion through Christ Jesus, as revealed to us in the given word of God.
   Put it on!

CHAPTER 05

THE SWORD OF THE SPIRIT

The sword of the spirit is not the written word as it were, but the spoken Word of God. In as much as the Bible is God's Word, it is of no effect or consequence to anyone's life, until it is lifted from the literal form into the spoken Word. It was the spoken Word Jesus called spirit and life not the written scriptures, which they had always had with them.

It is the Spirit who gives life; the flesh profits nothing. The words that I speak to you are spirit, and they are life...John6:63.

Using the Bible as a lining under the pillow guarantees no victory over demonic oppression. Having the Word in your spirit and out of your mouth is the real deal. No matter how many times you hit a man with the

Bible, it cannot bring salvation but will only leave him with some bruises. But if you preach the Word of salvation to an unsaved soul, light for salvation will follow the entrance of the word. In same way, if you start speaking God's word into any situation, change is guaranteed. Jesus said the words that he spoke were spirit and life not the word he wrapped in a fancy Bible wrapper.

For "whoever calls on the name of the LORD shall be saved." How then shall they call on Him in whom they have not believed? And how shall they believe in Him of whom they have not heard? And how shall they hear without a preacher? And how shall they preach unless they are sent? As it is written: "How beautiful are the feet of those who preach the gospel of peace, which bring glad tidings of good thing But they have not all obeyed the gospel. For Isaiah says, "LORD, who has believed our report?" So then faith comes by hearing, and hearing by the word of God. But I say, have they not heard? Yes indeed: "Their sound has gone out to all the earth and their words to the ends of the world"...Romans 10: 13-17

It is only the word given the vocal expression by a saved man, who is essentially a Spirit that qualifies to be called Sword of the Spirit. There is no mystical power in the Bible as a book; Christianity is not cultism or witchcraft where you need to conjure things. In book form, the Bible does not look different or feel different from any other book other than what the reader makes of it. This is where religious folks miss it a great deal. Many will hold the Bible and shout that it is the Sword of the Spirit even though they hardly know what is written in it, talk less of speaking it out of their mouth as their reality. So they stay defeated even though they have a big Bible is in their hand, on their dressing table, and under their pillow. Touching the Bible does not give you power, maybe spiritual goose pimples!

Bowing down before the Bible or displaying it on the shelf has no spiritual meaning or connotation. Hanging the picture of a bearded man carrying cross, with or without rosary or heart sign, is not equal to having Jesus present in your situation. Jesus is only present in the spoken Word of faith. The conception and birth of Jesus was according to but not by the written word. The conception and birth of Christ was by the spoken word. It had been written by the prophet and read by the people for years that a virgin would conceive and give birth to Christ, but the conception took place when Mary received the spoken word the angel Gabriel brought from the presence of the Lord.

Now in the sixth month the angel Gabriel was sent by God to a city of Galilee named Nazareth, to a virgin betrothed to a man whose name was Joseph, of the house of David. The virgin's name was Mary. And having come in, the angel said to her, Rejoice, highly favoured one, the Lord is with you; blessed are you among women! But when she saw him, she was troubled at his saying, and considered what manner of greeting this was.

Then the angel said to her, Do not be afraid, Mary, for you have found favour with God. And behold, you will conceive in your womb and bring forth a Son, and shall call His name JESUS. He will be great, and will be called the Son of the Highest; and the Lord God will give Him the throne of His father David. And He will reign over the house of Jacob forever, and of His kingdom there will be no end. Then Mary said to the angel, how can this be, since I do not know a man?

And the angel answered and said to her, The Holy Spirit will come upon you, and the power of the Highest will overshadow you; therefore, also, that Holy One who is to be born will be called the Son of God. Now indeed, Elizabeth your relative has also conceived a son in her old age; and this is now the sixth month for her who was called barren. For with God nothing will be impossible. Then Mary said, Behold the maidservant of the Lord! Let it be to me <u>according to your word</u>. And the angel departed from her.

From the scripture above, we can see that Jesus was a product of the spoken word. When the Bible said in the Saint John's gospel that the word became flesh, it was the spoken word from God received by Mary and not the parchments and theological books the Pharisees and Sadducees were carrying around for arguments and to convict who next to stone to death.

We all know that Jesus is the solution to all of life's

problems and challenges. Nothing is impossible with him. But the question is how I get him on the scene of my war. Mere religious observation or exclamation would not do. You need to see how it was in the beginning, how he was manifested in Mary's womb in order to appear on earth as saviour to help mankind fight the battle of salvation.

But the righteousness of faith speaks in this way, "Do not say in your heart, 'Who will ascend into heaven?' (That is, to bring Christ down from above) or, "who will descend into the abyss?'" (That is, to bring Christ up from the dead). But what does it say? "The word is near you, in your mouth and in your heart" (that is, the word of faith which we preach)...Romans 10:6-6

Praying, waiting, and hoping for Christ to descend bodily in your room and have a private conversation with you and telling you in baritone things like "yeah, my son, or my daughter, I am here now, let us go and fight your battle" remains forever in the realm of spiritual fantasy and religious fairy tale. Hoping Christ will come out of the grave or visiting a grave side in Jerusalem for a solution to life's issues is spiritually futile and scripturally senseless. Jesus died and was raised already. "He is not here, he is raised" were the words spoken to people who went to the grave three days after his death about 2,000 years ago. What then a waste of time it is to be searching for his body or grave to pray with today.

God has not left us helpless on how to get Jesus, the solution provider for all issues of life, into our situations. How I wish you knew that you do not need anyone to fetch Jesus for you, for Christ himself is nearer to you than you can imagine.

How?

Word!

Which Word?

The spoken Word from your believing heart, even the very Word of faith as it is written!

The spoken Word is the sword that proceeds from your spirit. That is why it is called the Sword of the Spirit. When you receive God's Word, you receive it into your spirit. Just as natural food is stored in your stomach, the food of the Word is stored in your belly or spirit. Whenever your spirit recognizes the need to cut down the opposing forces in life's battle, the stored Word is what your spirit channels through your tongue verbally as the Sword of the Spirit to get the work done

Then I turned to see the voice that spoke with me. And having turned I saw seven golden lamp stands, and in the midst of the seven lamp stands One like the Son of Man, clothed with a garment down to the feet and girded about the chest with a golden band. His head and hair were white like wool, as white as snow, and His eyes like a flame

of fire; His feet were like fine brass, as if refined in a furnace, and His voice as the sound of many waters; He had in His right hand seven stars, out of His mouth went a sharp two-edged sword, and His countenance was like the sun shining in its strength...Revelations 1:12-16.

The above revelation gives a graphic description of Christ Jesus in his spirit or glorified form. Significantly pointed out there is the fact that the sharp two-edged sword went out of His mouth, which is the spirit of the spoken Word. The writer spoke of what the Lord was doing when he saw him. The Lord was speaking to him. Your tongue does not go out of your mouth when speaking, so the two-edged sword was not the tongue of the Lord. The two-edged sword was the spoken word proceeding from his mouth.

The Lord is a spirit being, just as you are a spirit being too, because as he is so are we in this word.

Essentially, the sword of the spirit as the spoken word is meant for battle. It is to pull down strong holds and to fight against whatever you detest in your territory as we saw the Lord promised to do here. He did not like certain things in his Kingdom, so he said he was going to fight them with the sword or the word of his mouth

Repent, or else I will come to you quickly and will fight against them with the sword of my mouth...Revelation 2:16.

Even the Lord fights with the sword of his mouth, which as seen above, is the spoken word from his mouth. He had a few things against them and how did he do it? By the sword of the mouth, this is the spoken Word.

Then said I: Ah, Lord GOD! Behold, I cannot speak, for I am a youth. But the LORD said to me: do not say, I am a youth, for you shall go to all to whom I send you, and whatever I command you, you shall speak. Do not be afraid of their faces, for I am with you to deliver you, says the LORD. Then the LORD put forth His hand and touched my mouth, and the LORD said to me: Behold, I have put my words in your mouth. See, I have this day set you over the nations and over the kingdoms, to root out and to pull down, to destroy and to throw down, to build and to plant...Jeremiah1:6-10

The Lord will have Jeremiah pull down root out and destroy evil in his territory. The sword and bulldozer given to his hand were the word put in his mouth. Oh yes, the spoken Word from your spirit can pull down stronghold, cast down imagination, and destroy the cancer. Spoken word can paralyze the opposing force, cast the demons, defend the job, and save the marriage. Words do not speak themselves. You have to speak them with no shame or doubt, no embarrassment or apology.

Your tongue is not the two-edged sword. Your Bible is not the two-edged sword. The word written in the

Bible, which resides in your spirit, but spoken through your tongue against the opposition is the two-edged sword given to your spirit to fight and win with.

The significant thing about the Lord's sword is that it is sharp not dull. There is, therefore, a sharpness and fierceness expected in your word when using the sword. When speaking of defeat, unbelief, gossip, and swearing, many believers sadly have some very sharp stuff to deliver. A very sharp "sword of the flesh" to pull down possibilities and cast down victory and destroy others in mere criticisms guarantees you no victory in life. Do away with them.

When it is about healing, being healthily, prosperous, being above not beneath, and other good things of life that accompany salvation, the sword of the spirit of many Christian is so dull. Very drab, quite uncertain, and mostly kept in the sheath of their mouth in order not to rock the boat of religion, offend the society, and ultimately to let the devil like a sleeping dog lie, so to say. Suddenly you start hearing stuff like "I am not saying am a saint," but "I am a realist." Nothing is real in the material reality as mentioned earlier that it is not subject to change. A true realist sees the things already done and accomplished in the spirit as God the Eternal one puts them, he believes and call them because to him they are a present reality. They are real and never changing just like God who set them in place. Folks say things that magnify what they are going through at times to feel the emotional satisfaction and pleasure of venting the pressure. It is like a fix for the itch, it can give you the rush and win you some pity, but it never brings home the victory.

Conflict Of Swords

Looking through Biblical chronicles of battles, the battle between David and Goliath stands out. But David did not kill Goliath with any other thing than the sword of the spirit. The sling and the stones were just the outward manifestation of the battle already won by David in the spirit. The stature of Goliath or his armour was not what took the gas off the engine of Saul and his army but rather his demonic sword of the spirit. You need to also know that the devil deals in counterfeits arm-twisting and copy-catisim.

Then he stood and cried out to the armies of Israel, and said to them, why have you come out to line up for battle? Am I not a Philistine, and you the servants of Saul? Choose a man for yourselves, and let him come down to me. If he is able to fight with me and kill me, then we will be your servants. But if I prevail against him and kill him, then you shall be our servants and serve us. And the Philistine said, I defy the armies of Israel this day; give me a man, that we may fight together. When Saul and all Israel heard these words of the Philistine, they were dismayed and greatly afraid… 1 Samuel 17:8-11.

The children of Israel, having being in battle with Philistine over time, were not unfamiliar with giants.

They had seen all kinds from the first day they stepped into the Promised Land even as spies. No wonder the Bible never said they were afraid when they saw him. They were only afraid after hearing the words from his mouth. He pierced them and cast them down with his evil sword of the spirit. Goliath was using the evil sharp sword to cut them down. All they could muster was some dull drab sword of the flesh saying things like… 'Do you see how bad the situation is, we are in deep trouble now, let us just surrender to limit the damage at least' …no wonder they could not bring Goliath down. Verse 33 said they were in dread after seeing the man Goliath, but they only saw him in the light of what he was saying. Every time Goliath came, he did not only walk down the aisle as a model for them to appreciate his stature and armour. He came to say things, to cut them down, pierce their confidence, and cast down their winning imagination.

Friends, I know this is the copy cat satanic strategy of old. He clothes his own with his evil armour, including the sword of the spirit or spoken word. In order to deflate you, paralyse your imaginations, and cast you down from the lofty mountain of the dreamers where all things are possible. Some of you have heard stories or words from others that take gas off your engine of possibility for too long. It is high time you started refuelling using your own sword or word also. The good news is you have a sharper sword in God. It is sharper than any other sword. David knew this and he brought down Goliath. As Goliath was releasing his satanic sword from the realm of darkness, David was also releasing the sword of God from the realm of light, and the light shone in darkness so much that the darkness could not withstand it.

And when the Philistine looked about and saw David, he disdained him; for he was only a youth, ruddy and good-looking. So the Philistine said to David, "Am I a dog that you come to me with sticks?" And the Philistine cursed David by his gods. And the Philistine said to David, "Come to me, and I will give your flesh to the birds of the air and the beasts of the field!" Then David said to the Philistine, "You come to me with a sword, with a spear, and with a javelin. But I come to you in the name of the LORD of hosts, the God of the armies of Israel, whom you have defied. This day the LORD will deliver you into my hand, and I will strike you and take your head from you. And this day I will give the carcasses of the camp of the Philistines to the birds of the air and the wild beasts of the earth, that all the earth may know that there is a God in Israel. Then all this assembly shall know that the LORD does not save with sword and spear; for the battle is the LORD's, and He will give you into our hands."...1 Samuel 17:42-47.

The same bluffing and threat from the giant, same quit-notice on their lives from a deadly one called Goliath. The same words from force of darkness carrying negative influence were directed toward them, leaders and followers alike. Saul and his army heard the same words from Goliath and saw an insurmountable man-mountain. David came under the same sword of words from Goliath, but rather than surrendering to despair, the sword of the wicked provoked him to draw his own sword of light from within. Often, agonising from the pain and bleeding you sustain from the evil sword of the wicked targeted at you may make you forget you have a sharper sword, too.

My assignment is to make you see the potency in your own sword and implore you to deploy same for your incontrovertible victory.

Many have read the economy of the World so much that they cannot see or say anything else than recession, redundancy, lack, and woes. Having studied the medical report given to them so much that they cannot imagine overcoming the health problem, they start saying things contrary to what they really want. There is this funny good feeling that comes out of speaking defeat and helplessness. It is like venting anger with words and actions even when you know it is destructive, counterproductive, and spiritually unwise to do so. The truth is that you do not need to start boasting or laying claim to high and lofty things in the face of challenges, but you can start from where you are, declaring what God has done before and what he can do now even when it does not fit in or feel right with your fleshly feelings. This goes beyond positive confession. This is bringing out the sword from the inside of your spirit man based on your walking with God in the light of the written word.

But David said to Saul, "Your servant used to keep his father's sheep, and when a lion or a bear came and took a lamb out of the flock, I went out after it and struck it, and delivered the lamb from its mouth; and when it arose against me, I caught it by its beard, and struck and killed it. Your servant has killed both lion and bear; and this uncircumcised Philistine will be like one of them, seeing he has defied the armies of the living God." Moreover David said, "The LORD, who delivered me from the paw of the lion and from the paw of the bear, He will deliver me from the hand of this Philistine…" 1 Samuel 17:34-37

David did not say he had fought Goliath before or anyone like him. All he did was just look at what the Lord can do and he kept saying it, corroborating it with what the Lord had done before. If the Lord could save you from sin, He is able to save you from sickness also. If God had kept you till now, He can keep you till old age. These were the kind of swords champions use.

I will kill this also, David said!

The Lord will deliver me from this also. If I can go through school and come out in spite of all the odds out there, I will get a good job also no matter what the economy says. If I can get married by his grace, I will have children also. If I can leave drunkenness behind, I can leave immorality in any shade, too. If I can quit this, I am able to also quit that. The champion's sword is the sword of light sharpened against the wiles of the devil.

May I say this friend: **sharp saints use sharp swords.** When you are among folks and they keep talking of defeat, troubles, how impossible it is to break even, how difficult it is to come out of the troubles at hand, engage your sharp sword by speaking sharp words from your sharp spirit and keep speaking it. Let them mock you and read meaning to your words and motive. They will still be there when you are bringing Goliath's head back home, manifesting the star in you.

I see your star rising in Jesus' name. I employ the sword of my mouth now against the mountain before you right now. I speak against your Goliath and I declare them moved and destroyed for your sake in Jesus' mighty name...amen.

Sword Is In Sizes

And a champion went out from the camp of the Philistines, named Goliath, from Gath, whose height was six cubits and a span. He had a bronze helmet on his head, and he was armed with a coat of mail, and the weight of the coat was five thousand shekels of bronze. And he had bronze armour on his legs and a bronze javelin between his shoulders. Now the staff of his spear was like a weaver's beam and his iron spearhead weighed six hundred shekels; and a shield-bearer went before him

If you look closely at Goliath's armour, you will notice that his sword, in particular, was proportional to his stature. In the things of the spirit, your sword tells us your spirit size as well. Hope you know your word is your sword!

When you hear people talk like grasshoppers, it is because they are grasshoppers within or in their spirit. When you hear folks like Caleb and Joshua speak like giants who could do anything, it is because they were giants inside with the giant's sword proceeding from their mouth on the outside. A giant sword might be mistaken for arrogance and boastfulness, but the assessment and testimony of God differs indeed.

Then they told him, and said: "We went to the land where you sent us. It truly flows with milk and honey, and this is its fruit. Nevertheless the people who dwell in the land are strong; the cities are fortified and very large; moreover we saw the descendants of Anak there. The Amalekites dwell in the land of the South; the Hittites, the Jebusites, and the Amorites dwell in the mountains; and the Canaanites dwell by the sea and along the banks of the Jordan." Then Caleb quieted the people before Moses, and said, Let us go up at once and take possession, for we are well able to overcome it." But the men who had gone up with him said, We are not able to go up against the people, for they are stronger than we. And they gave the children of Israel a bad report of the land which they had spied out, saying, The land through which we have gone as spies is a land that devours its inhabitants, and all the people whom we saw in it are men of great stature. There we saw the giants (the descendants of Anak came from the giants); and we were like grasshoppers in our own sight, and so we were in their sight...Numbers 13:27-33

Joshua and Caleb were not just giving a positive confession in order to sound spiritual. They were passionate about what they were saying. It was a sword drawn from their innermost being. No one was trying to convince or encourage them to stay positive. They were really positive. They could not see it in any other way or any other form. The swords of Joshua and Caleb were not copied nor downloaded from someone or somewhere. It wasn't a rhyme they were reciting trying to convince themselves about the validity of their declarations. Joshua and Caleb had giants' swords born out of a passionate giant spirit. 'Another spirit' God called their well-built giant spirit.

But Joshua the son of Nun and Caleb the son of Jephunneh, who were among those who had spied out the land, tore their clothes; and they spoke to all the congregation of the children of Israel, saying: The land we passed through to spy out is an exceedingly good land. If the LORD delights in us, then He will bring us into this land and give it to us, a land which flows with milk and honey.

Only do not rebel against the LORD, nor fear the people of the land, for they are our bread; their protection has departed from them, and the LORD is with us. Do not fear them.

The passion seen in Caleb and Joshua was born out their persons. They were giants within, so they could not be grasshoppers without. Just because the tide looked like turning against them was not enough to keep them silent. They were giants within and would rather die as giants than to live as grasshoppers. Funny enough, divine judgement said they will live and the grasshoppers would die. Come to think of it, which king will take grasshoppers to battle as the elite army to represent his kingdom. God was not ready to lose his battle, so he chose not to go with the grasshoppers or be the commander of grasshopper troop.

People exempt God from the battles they are fighting most times unknowingly with all kind of things they say.
Then the LORD said: I have pardoned, according to your word; but truly, as I live, all the earth shall be filled with the glory of the LORD— because all these men who have seen My glory and the signs which I did in Egypt and in the wilderness, and have put Me to the test now these ten times, and have not heeded My voice, they certainly shall not see the land of which I swore to their fathers, nor shall any of those who rejected Me see it. But my servant Caleb, because he has a different spirit in him and has followed me fully, I will bring into the

land where he went, and his descendants shall inherit it...Numbers 14:20-24.

Get Your Sword Ready

Sharpening your sword is your responsibility as a warrior of the spirit. But in as much as your words are your sword, your utmost concern is not your mouth but the source of your word. It is possible to profess positive confessions till your mouth bleeds and yet lose the battle. Many get so caught up with the positive confession craze but keep wondering why defeat is still staring them in the face. Let us examine this closely.

Death and life are in the power of the tongue, and those who love it will eat its fruit...Proverbs 18:21

Taking a verse of scripture and stretching it out of context can cause an accident. In as much as the tongue is shown above as the channel through which death or life is channelled, we can also see that the channel and the source are different.

Keep your heart with all diligence, for out of it spring the issues of life...Proverbs 4:23

The tap can be turn on and off to let out the water, but the tap is not the source of the water. Turning a tap connected to an empty reservoir is not just futile but foolish. As important as the tongue is when it comes to issue of life, the Bible did not ask you to lay emphasis there and there alone because the power of life channelled through tongue does not originate from the tongue.

The good man brings good things out of the good stored up in his heart, and the evil man brings evil things out of the evil stored up in his heart. For out of the overflow of his heart his mouth speaks…Luke 6:45 (NIV)

The three scriptures above show us the way out of the spirit sword issue. The mouth can only speak when the heart or the spirit has it. The Bible never said the flow is from mouth to heart. The Bible admonishes you to guard your heart. Jesus speaking with the religious bigots of his days put it succinctly and emphatically that the things of the spirit cannot be successfully faked or made up. In the days of adversity it would not work, and of course it is a matter of time before the result shows what is inside. The 10 elders we saw earlier too made some positive confessions… the land is good, flowing with milk and honey they said… but time tested their heart and they soon started saying what was within them in deed. Stop playing church. Pay attention to your inner man and feed him. The size of your inner man is your true size. It also determines the size of your sword. The sharpness of your spirit determines the sharpness of your sword. Sharpen up within. The word within determines the sword without.

<u>Store It Up, Sword It Out</u>

The whole armour was described as the whole armour of God in the beginning of this book, with the sword included. No wonder it is called the sword of the spirit knowing full well that God is a spirit. When I therefore say your word is your sword, the onus is on you to make the word of God your word if the sword of God will be your sword.

Luke 6:45 in the New International version above clearly shows that there is a conscious storing expected of you. When the word is stored in your heart, it will flow though your mouth or tongue.

The good man brings good things out of the good stored up in his heart…Luke 6:45a (NIV).

This good man was not just bringing out of nothing. This good man did the home work of storing. He was not just wishing he stored. The stored words in time of peace become the sword word readily available for battle in time of war.

Concluding this chapter let me admonish you with this word.

Let the word of Christ dwell in you richly in all wisdom, teaching and admonishing one another in psalms and hymns and spiritual songs, singing with grace in your hearts to the Lord…Colossians 3:16.

Yinka Akintunde

CHAPTER 06

SHEILD THOSE DARTS OFF

Above all, taking the shield of faith with which you will be able to quench all the fiery darts of the wicked one...Ephesians 6:16.

Above all, what a phrase to start with, Whenever a list is given of what to do and you are told that above all do this, what it means is that all the others will not likely work unless you do all of the tasks above. Talking about victory in the face of life's challenges, faith is an above-all weapon. It is the spice of faith that gives taste and value to whatever you are cooking for victory in the kingdom. Whenever resistance comes up against your forward movement, what you need above any other thing is faith.

I love the word "all" in this verse. It shows that faith is a do-it-all medicine, all-conquering weapon, no limitation or exception. Nothing escapes faith. There is no dart of life thrown at you by the devil that will not bow to Bible faith. All darts are quenchable by faith no matter how fiery. Oh yes, I know how terrible and devastating life's battles can be even with a believer. Many uninvited troubles get shot at us, many unenvisaged challenges come our way even having done all and taken all the right stands for standing. The winning way is not by explaining the victory away, not by crying all night long, even though there might not be anything wrong with venting emotion through crying as long as you do the right thing to fix the trouble when you finish crying. The only and godly acceptable disposition you need toward your trouble is to quench it, not back out.

No matter how wicked the arrows thrown at you are, you are to quench it, no matter what area of your life, you are to quench or kill it. Growths in your body, a leakage in your purse, storm in your career boat, all are darts thrown at you to stop your joy. You are not admonished and cannot afford to live with them. Quench the darts. No matter how bad the darts, God's plan and purpose for you is to win but victory is not guaranteed until faith is at work.

Faith releases divine ability wherewith you can fight and win "Wherewith ye shall be able to quench all the fairy darts of the devil." Most folks erroneously think that faith for victory is a reserved privileged ability possessed mysteriously by some strong Christians, but the irony is faith rather makes any Christian strong by imbibing such with the ability and wherewithal such did not have until the faith comes.

For whatever is born of God overcomes the world. And this is the victory that has overcome the world—our faith...1 John 5:4

Faith is not a doctrine. It is not optional. It is not one of the things you need in life. It is the very thing you need. I have heard people mocking faith preaching and teachings, but looking closely at such doctrinal bigots, nothing worth emulating oozes out from their lives or ministries. Faith is not a movement. Offering collections and fund raisings on television are not same and equal with faith preaching or teaching. In fact, reducing faith to "name it and claim it" is reducing the precious mountain of victory and dominion to a cheap mould out of which nothing significant in exploit could be gotten.

Faith is the "above all other things weapon," a universal currency against all the fiery darts of the enemy. The Bible did not say this is one of the victories or this is a significant part of the victory. Rather the Bible calls faith **the victory**, which invariably means that no matter how sincere you are at the battle front of life, no matter how much of the other things you are carrying, the victory is still hinged on your faith walk. When you are fighting one as wicked as Satan, even though the Lord had fatally knock him down in your behalf, to take your victorious spoil of war and keep him down where he belongs, you need divine ability. What faith does for you is to enable you or grant you the divine ability to keep him down, knowing full well that it took divine ability through our Lord Jesus Christ to knock him down in the first place.

The word "whatsoever" in the above scripture can be interpreted as "whosoever" in this context, which means victory is not an exclusive right of some, but a heritage of everyone born of God. If victory is guaranteed only through faith, it then becomes a must have for all aspiring to make their victory a reality.

Take It Up

...taking the shield of faith...

What do you do with faith in conflicts of life? You are to take it as shield. No one can take it for you. Your pastor can pray for you or prophecy on you as a help in your faith walk. But when it comes to being shielded from the darts flying around from the wicked one, you need to take your own shield faith. Jesus was Peter's pastor, a very worded, powerful and anointed one for that matter. But when it came to the battle of life, the master knew it would take Peter's faith for Peter to win so he guided his intercession for Peter in the right direction.

Simon, Simon, Satan has asked to sift you as wheat.

But I have prayed for you, Simon that your faith may not fail. And when you have turned back, strengthen your brothers."...Luke22:31

If laying on of hand was the way out, Jesus would have done just that. If sowing a special seed of money was, Peter would have been sent to the river to quickly get enough seed from fish mouth probably. But to quench this fiery dart, Peter needed to take his shield of faith and so Jesus prayed the right prayer of intercession for him that in taking it he would not fail. If he had failed to take the shield of faith, his failure would have been thorough and permanent. The attack was nothing short of fiery. Satan wanted to beat Peter small like wheat reducing his life to mere chaff, but faith won.

Maybe you are going through issues that have barely taken all the good substance off you, threatening to leave your life in ruins and tatters with nothing remaining to live for. I have good news for you. The shield of faith will do and I pray for you at this moment that your faith will be strengthened and not fail. The attack left Peter and everyone around him so weak that the master said after the victory is won, a special attention should be paid to strength. Maybe the events of life have left you weak and even feeble to the point of dropping down. My assignment to you at this point is to encourage you to muster the last strength in you just to take this shield of faith. You may be dying but take it, paralysed kindly take it, broken, busted, and dejected please take the shield. This might be the last ounce of energy you can muster. I am not asking you to try it but I am asking you to take it. Take it and see the victory of the Lord and the weakness of the fiery one attacking you. The enemy himself knows how potent your shield of faith is and how he will not have a choice but to flee once you take it, so he goes all the way to abuse your mind and weaken your hand in other to stop you from doing so and winning him.

See what the word says:

Therefore submit to God. Resist the devil and he will flee from you…James 4:7.

How am I to resist the devil, you ask, since I can see that he will flee if I muster enough courage to do just that?

See what the word says again:

Be sober; be vigilant; because your adversary the devil walks about like a roaring lion, seeking whom he may devour. Resist him, steadfast in the faith, knowing that the same sufferings are experienced by your brotherhood in the world…1 Peter 5:8-9.

Peter being a veteran in the warfare, having being the centre of fierce attack of the wicked one before, was inspired by the Holy Spirit of God to show you how to successfully resist the devil to the point of him fleeing is her clearly delivering the message. Resist the adversary with steadfast faith, simple!

Take the shield to resist him, he cannot but flee, there is no other way; the eternal reality or truth is that he will flee. No matter how much noise he is making now, no matter how deep seated he seems established in the issue and no matter how long he has been on it, the present pain and shame irrespective, take up the shield he will eventually flee.

Grow Your Shield

The size of a warrior determines the size of shield he carries. Therefore the size of your destiny to be accomplished, the level of your vision and how much you want out in life can be reflected through your shield size. This is simply so because the greater the bout, the greater the glory, which invariably means the fiercer the darts or blow to deal with. Little bout comes with little blows and invariably defended with a little shield. It is therefore needful to grow your shield if you are asking more from life knowing full well that your faith is your shield in the days of darts.

Many people wonder why we lay emphasis on growing your faith. The simple reason is that the size of arrow a masked man will throw at an elephant for a kill is not same for a squirrel. The devil is a wicked masked man. When he sees greatness in your future and your destiny, he gets mad and starts throwing all kinds of darts at you. He targets your health, finances, home, ministry, children, and relatives to cause a stalemate and distraction in your pursuit of such greatness. Friend, you will need a sizeable shield for the sizeable darts, a fiery faith for the fiery dart, and a steadfast shield of faith for the steadfast roaring of the wicked.

For the purpose of our discussion, I will simply highlight the three principal ways to grow your faith as a shield against any size of dart the enemy throws at you:

(i)   Word as Seed and Water

So then faith comes by hearing, and hearing by the word of God…Romans 10:17.

The word of God is the primary precursor of faith, the very fibre with which faith is built. Faith is not a strong will or strong head. Faith is not positive thinking as it were. Faith is the substance or fruit that comes to the human spirit when the word of God finds an entrance into the heart and is allowed to germinate therein as seed.

Just like a natural seed needs water to grow, when the word-seed is sown to produce faith in the heart, the water needed to grow it is also the word of God. So faith comes by hearing, and hearing by the word of God…while some will be the seed, some will be the water watering the seed. If, for example, a seed of the word in finances is sown in your heart and it produces faith to fight the fiery dart of poverty, as the seed is growing producing faith as shield in the face of your numerous financial needs, you need more word in that same light to keep watering the seed so that fruit of faith or the shield may not wither or dry up but rather grow till it quench the fiery darts of lack and want in your life.

The reality is that the fiery darts of the wicked on an issue will momentarily increase once the enemy knows you are putting up a resistance and challenging the status quo. The only victorious choice you have is to fortify your shield of faith more until it quenches the darts. The primary way of doing so is to water the truth believing faith in you with more truth. You need to bear in mind that the word that produces faith is the word of God and not just anything literally quoted from the Bible. The word of God here refers to the revelation of the eternal plan, purpose, promises, and provisions of God for us through Christ as revealed in the scripture.

(ii)   The Exercise of Faith

And the apostles said to the Lord, "Increase our faith." So the Lord said, "If you have faith as a mustard seed, you can say to this mulberry tree, 'Be pulled up by the roots and be planted in the sea,' and it would obey you. And which of you, having a servant ploughing or tending sheep, will say to him when he has come in from the field, 'Come at once and sit down to eat'? But will he not rather say to him, 'Prepare something for my supper, and gird yourself and serve me till I have

eaten and drunk, and afterward you will eat and drink'? Does he thank that servant because he did the things that were commanded him? I think not. So likewise you, when you have done all those things which you are commanded, say, 'We are unprofitable servants. We have done what was our duty to do.

The very simple request of the apostles here was for Christ to increase their faith. Christ, not wanting to deceive them, showed them that it takes personal responsibility for faith to increase. He could have cajoled them and started a spiritual gimmick, but not the Lord. He showed them the way by using two illustrations to explain same principle. Looking at the question again, all they asked for was an increase in faith. Most certainly they had seen the exploits of faith with the master, and he went on and on to tell them of a master and his servant, which to a casual reader sounds incongruous with the issue at hand. A closer look at the scripture will first show us that all you need for a great faith is to have a small one first - not just have it but use it. Faith in this context is belief, which you possess in your heart having heard the word of God. Having faith as small as mustard seed was not the crucial issue here because having faith as small as a mustard seed was not the apostles' problem. Increasing the size of that small faith was the issue. Jesus identified the real work as using that small faith when the need arises as the Herculean task needed to increase it. How will they start this use? The Lord said by speaking the faith as word, saying to the challenges at hand without

shame or adding but, not observing what becomes of their words or waiting to see it works or not.
This same principle is called the spirit or attitude of faith.

And since we have the same spirit of faith, according to what is written, "I believed and therefore I spoke," we also believe and therefore speak...2 Corinthians 4:13

You cannot believe and not voice it out. This is not a positive confession, but taking responsibility as a spiritual warrior. It is not optional. It has nothing to do with your nature as many will have us believe. They do not like talking and so making faith declaration is out of place for them. There is no introvert in the school of faith! There probably were introverts among the apostles, too. But the Lord Jesus said for faith to grow, such an introvert must open his mouth and speak of the mustard seed faith as well. Here the Lord was not just asking them to blab. He said speaking of faith is saying to this mountain, specific words targeted at specific issues not vague words spoken out of uncertainty for the sake of speaking them. He then went ahead to illustrate that the responsibility to grow your faith goes beyond mere declaration of the word but doing what the word says. The servant's duty was to do what was commanded of him, which ultimately will be to his benefit. This is what the phrase "we are unprofitable" means. When we act on God's word or divine commandment, we could erroneously think we are doing God a favour. But Christ said it is not so but we are rather growing our faith, which is to our benefits. From the two illustrations given as answer to the question by the Lord, we can then conclude that either by saying or by doing, taking responsible corresponding action with your little faith is what guarantees growth of same.

To grow your shield, putting it to use is the wisdom. Don't hide it, pretending as if you don't love victory or fearing you may fail or what will people say if it does not work. Spiritual principles are universal currencies. The Lord knew all the "ifs" and all the probable probability on Earth before belching this rule out of eternity. If faith will grow faith has to be exercised like muscle. At times, it could be painfully rigorous and tiring but the attending development and evolvement is worth the rigours.

(iii)   Build On It

But you, beloved, building yourselves up on your most holy faith, praying in the Holy Spirit...Jude 20.

The reason why praying in the spirit will build or increase your stand in your faith is not farfetched.

For he who speaks in a tongue does not speak to men but to God, for no one understands him; however, in the spirit he speaks mysteries...1 Corinthians 14:2.

So all prayers are not communicating with God, which is understandable, but when you pray in the spirit, which simply means praying in tongues, you are said to be speaking to God. The truth is when you speak to God enough; he will speak back to you. God is a spirit. He communicates to your spirit as well, and when his word comes to you, what the word produces in you will be faith.

The gift of faith is a ministry gift given when you need to function well in certain offices as you minister to people. This gift is called the gift of the spirit, referring to God's spirit. The more you stay with God in fellowship, the more the gift flows. No matter how much you love someone, gifts can only be given when there is access to them. When you are consistently praying in the spirit, you are simply creating access for a flow of gifts and building up your house of faith. You are fortifying your shield. No wonder you are always bold and fearless when you take time to fellowship with God in prayer, daring the most wicked of all evil darts. Can you imagine if you make this a lifestyle? Your shield will be strong, ever increasing, shining - one quenching all darts of the wicked no matter how fierce.

Nice But Fighting

Polite language is not commonly heard among soldiers in the battle front. The enemy does not announce the coming of the dart. He is called the wicked one, so faith is not a church services item you put on as a robe on Sunday. Faith is not a pass into the elite club or clique of the church. Faith is the dart quenching shield you confront challenges of life with.

In warfare, no matter how well trained or how devastating you are in bringing the opposition down, you need to still be shielded against the flying darts or you might not last long on the battle front. A strong bullet in the head from a sniper will do total and fatal damage and that is the end, even though you are well trained. Once the shield is out of place or out of size, you are left exposed to all kinds of darts flying around.

Among the great men in the Bible who performed great exploits were Shadrach, Meshach, and Abednego. They were not bad people. They were not illiterate or lazy, yet fiery darts were thrown at them. They were knowledgeable and skilful, but the fiery dart shot at them did not answer to skills and didn't answer to their mental excellence. Have you not come across skilful folks, talented people, and people with all kinds of degrees, yet the darts of the wicked are chasing them? The wicked one has no respect for good looks, academic achievements, or skills. If those three Hebrew boys had not gotten what it takes to quench it, they would have been killed and nothing would have happened.

Oh, many have innocently fallen victim to the wicked darts of the devil and yet life continues. In eternity, if the play back is shown to many they will see that, though not fair, many of the life's battles they ultimately lost were winnable. Until the three Hebrew boys came on the scene, no one ever challenged the king's authority or of survived the fire of his judgement. The majority would have thrown a pity party or staged a protest against God, asking why them, but they still would have been destroyed by the wicked all the same.

I pray you have what it takes to answer when the wicked one knocks. Amen!

It is a matter of when the wicked one will always shoot the fiery darts. It comes as naturally to him as breathing. That is why he is called the wicked one in the first place. People have preached and written books trying to explain why bad things happen to **"good"** people, but the answer is simple, **"the wicked one."** He is the thrower of the fiery darts.

No matter how much analysis you do, a headache is still an ache, and if it is aches badly, what you need is relief, not an explanation. Eloquent preaching is good only if it produces faith. Exegesis is great only if it produces faith. Talented and skilful performances on the pulpit are fine as long as they produce faith because when the wicked one comes around to steal, kill, and destroy, faith is the only antidote proven and recommended in the Bible to defeat the moves.

The famed fiery furnace was quenched through faith.

Were they good people?

Yes!

Were they hardworking, well-educated, and holy people?

Yes!

But what quenched the fiery darts thrown at them?

Faith!

And what more shall I say? For the time would fail me to tell of Gideon and Barak and Samson and Jephthah, also of David and Samuel and the prophets: who through faith subdued kingdoms, worked righteousness, obtained promises, stopped the mouths of lions, quenched the violence of fire...Hebrews 11:32-34a.

For the sake of time, a summary of exploits was listed in the Bible with attributes to faith at work, quenching the violence of fire including the three Hebrew boys.

The Christian call is to be a soldier. It is in your nature to be nice, but it is also your duty and call to fight.

Quench These Flames, Stop These Darts

The flames of fire do not quench themselves, not the fiery ones aimed at you in particular. It is your responsibility to quench them. Whatever your attitude toward life will only leave the fiery flame burning to the consuming state of devastation. It takes a decided effort to quench it. The Hebrew boys' offense was that they stood for something. Is it not funny that in life you do not come against stiff resistance until you start to take action against the status quo? To go along with the flow is always the easiest route in life - nothing to be distinct in, nothing extraordinary in finances, career, or health. Become sick like other people and die if possible. Join other losers in the market place of life to talk about how cruel life is and how unconcerned God is with the plight of mankind. It is very easy to sit down and complain, criticize, and analyze, but to effect change as a result of standing for what you know and are convinced of is another ball game reserved only for winners by choice.

The three Hebrew boys stood for something. They choose not to fall like a pack of cards along with other spineless folks. The Hebrew boys did not fear failing or loosing, but they would not do so without putting up a fight, a real fight for that matter. Before folks start talking of impossibility and blaming everyone and everything, I wish they would identify the dart of the wicked one causing them the pain and put up a good fight of faith first.

Fight the good fight of faith, lay hold on eternal life, to which you were also called and have confessed the good confession in the presence of many witnesses...1 Timothy6:12.

You are admonished not to go down just like that. There is nothing in store for men who just go down without laying hold of anything substantial. But when you fight a good fight, you will definitely lay hold of victory. You will kill the tumour and lay hold of your health. You will kill the poverty and lay hold of your wealth. You will destroy the opposition and lay hold of success in your career and family, but you need to fight. Fight like the three Hebrew boys fought who by faith committed God into their battle.

Commit God- And Care Less

Shadrach, Meshach, and Abed-Nego answered and said to the king, "O Nebuchadnezzar, we have no need to answer you in this matter. If that is the case, our God whom we serve is able to deliver us from the burning fiery furnace, and He will deliver us from your hand, O king. But if not, let it be known to you, O king, that we do not serve your gods, nor will we worship the gold image which you have set up…Daniel 3:14-18.

Committing God through faith puts the opposition in a dangerous position against God who cannot be defeated. It is wonderful to know that as a Christian, you can actually commit God to your battle and He will show up. The Hebrew boys cared less how the opposition saw their standing. All the same they stood. Jesus' teaching on the mount exposed how care and anxiety will take God out of a man's battle pronto.

So why do you worry about clothing? Consider the lilies of the field, how they grow: they neither toil nor spin; and yet I say to you that even Solomon in all his glory was not arrayed like one of these. Now if God so clothes the grass of the field, which today is, and tomorrow is thrown into the oven, will He not much more clothe you, O you of little faith? Therefore do not worry, saying, "What shall we eat?" or "What shall we drink?" or "What shall we wear?" For after all these things the Gentiles seek. For your heavenly Father knows that you need all these things…Mathew 6: 28 -32

Jesus is simply saying that there are things you cannot do by yourself, but there are still things you can do. God is not expecting you to do that which you are not equipped to do. Faith is taking responsibility in doing that which you are meant to do thereby committing God to do what he alone can do. Faith puts God on the scene to do that which he alone can do. For example, Jesus said the ability to add a cubit to your stature without a knife lies with God. Why then beat yourself up about it?

Apostle Paul writing to the Philippians said if you want God on the scene of your battles. Get rid of that care. It is borne out of the sin of unbelief. But if you will commit God, he will garrison your heart (battle ground of life) against the onslaught of the wicked.

Be anxious for nothing, but in everything by prayer

and supplication, with thanksgiving, let your requests be made known to God; and the peace of God, which surpasses all understanding, will guard your hearts and minds through Christ Jesus…Philippians 4:6-7.

Faith literally puts God on the scene of your battle when you commit him by getting rid of care and anxiety, which simply points to unbelief or is interpreted as you saying that I want to or I can do it alone. I have heard people paint unbelief in diverse eloquent and glorious ways. "You know I am just being careful, I am a perfectionist you know." most of the time, most of these assertions point to care and anxiety born out of unbelief.

The Hebrew boys did not care what names they were called or how stupid they looked to critical observers. See how they confronted the problem they could see with a God they could not see. That is called faith. They were shielded from the anger they could feel with the love they could only believe.

Remember, faith puts God on the scene of your battle.

Big God, Able God

True faith puts divine ability on the line. These men were not talking of what they could do, but they saw an able God worthy of trust. They probably have never seen God deliver anyone like that before, but that still did not take anything away from His ability to do so if the need arose. The truth is, when you know how able God, is you can put anything on line trusting him.

All ability is resident in your God. He is able to do anything. Archaeology or science is too limited to intimidate or limit God. He is infallible. What God does or does not do is not what makes Him God. He is God because He is God, the self-existing one. This is where many people miss it in the school of faith. They think God is God because He does this or that, not all! He said, "I am," that is Him. The Hebrew boys understood this concept, so faith came to them. God has nothing to prove to anybody. If He does, then He ceases to be God. He is not answerable to anyone but himself, rather all will answer to Him. He does not have to please anybody but all must please Him and the only way to do that is the way of faith. Hebrews 11:6.

When God was pleased, He came on the scene. What killed man, of course, could not kill God's presence in the fire. The fourth man was said to be like a Son of God, a miniature or an off-shoot of God born by faith of men.

Will God do anything and fight all battles as long as I am involved?

Sadly no, God can do all things, but He does not. God's ability will only answer to your faith when you believe right. God appears weak or incapable in many situations believers go through in life, yet He is never weak or weary. God's power or divine abilities available for man's triumph are only packaged in the covenants of promises. So even though God is able to do all things, He only does what He promises. When you want to unleash God's ability through faith, you do not just close your eyes and take a plunge. No, you need a covenant of promises platform as your spring diving board and God will be down there to catch you.

He staggered not at the promise of God through unbelief; but was strong in faith, giving glory to God; and being fully persuaded that, what he had promised, he was able also to perform. Romans 4: 20 – 21.(KJV)

This scripture talks of Abraham who, in the face of all odds, trusted God and got results. His trust was not just some blind trust. His trusting God was promised-based. Faith only comes by God's Word, not by what I want. Many believers want God to do what He did not say and so their faiths do not work. For example, no anointing can fix a marriage when requisite character is lacking in either or both partners. There will always be chaos as long as the word responsibility is not taken. Ephesians 5:22-29. There is no level of believing that can make a lazy unproductive person wealthy forever. **Psalm 1:1–3; 1Thessalonians 3: 10.**

The Hebrew boys knew God promised His wrath to idolaters and His being God indeed to those who refuse idols Leviticus 9:4; 26: 1. I am the Lord your God, He said, and they knew "I am" was the same man of war who drowned Pharaoh and his host so they were never scared of another king's threats. The things, which were written afore time, served as an example by which they developed hope around which they built the tangible substance of their faith. When you take relevant promises on a subject matter and lay hold of them, they become your shield against whatever dart is coming out on such issue. Saying, I believe in God or I believe in the Bible is not going to do the job but laying hold of specific word and trusting God that He will stand as a man of war according to such word is the winning formula in the face of conflict.

Faith Attitude

For the rest of this chapter, I will show you some very crucial issues in the school of faith and I pray you will get it. When in place, faith toward God will be an ever-increasing way of life for you.

Faith primarily believes God's word of promise, trusting in his faithfulness of commitment to do it, and being persuaded of his ability to deliver at his own appointed time.

This was clearly seen in the household of Abraham who believed what God said. They judged God faithful to do what he said and were fully persuaded of his ability to do it. The real challenge that put Abraham and Sarah's faith on the spot was having the fruit of the womb. Many other people in the Bible had different challenges, which put their faith on the spot as well. Many won while others lost. Though the challenges were different from one person to another, so also was the expression of their faith or what they believed, said or did to effect changes. Yet the whole of Hebrew 11 said all of these divers believe, words, and actions were faith at work.

Our challenges in life will definitely be different just as we are probably serving on different battle front, though we are all in same army of the Lord fighting a common adversary. But the universal currency for everyone is faith. The difference in challenge may require that we believe different words, say different things to different mountains, and invariably take different actions. The ultimate denominator in the school of faith, therefore, is our faith attitude. Talking about battles, the naval troop on the turbulent Pacific and elite squad in the storm of the desert may be fighting the same war, representing same government yet aren't facing the same challenges, and thus won't take same action. But they will all need the same attitude to be victorious. Whatever you are fighting, if the attitude is there, the shield will show up.

but truly, as I live, all the earth shall be filled with the glory of the LORD— because all these men who have seen My glory and the signs which I did in Egypt and in the wilderness, and have put Me to the test now these ten times, and have not heeded My voice, they certainly shall not see the land of which I swore to their fathers, nor shall any of those who rejected Me see it. But my servant Caleb, because he has a different spirit in him and has followed me fully, I will bring into the land where he went, and his descendants shall inherit it...Numbers 14:21-24.

This was divine judgement after 12 men, including Joshua and Caleb, were sent to spy out the land of the giants. Ten excluding, the two named above, brought back an evil report and God said the difference was not the size of the problem they all saw but the attitude inherent in them.

Challenges are the true test of attitude because they provoke spontaneous inherent reaction, either of a winner or a loser. Another spirit here simply referred to another attitude. Many think God was talking about the Holy Spirit, which is also the Spirit of faith here but not at all. It will be contradictory to divine nature and justice to expect same reaction from 12 of them if the two mentioned had the Holy Spirit and the other 10 did not have same Holy Spirit. God was therefore talking about their own spirits or inner man. Knowing that they were in the image of the first Adam who was dead spiritually then, God could not be referring to their inner man or spirit man but rather their inner milieu or personality, their belief system, or attitude which matters a lot in the conflict of life. The subject of faith is essentially a vertical issue meaning that the faith that quenches the fiery dart of the devil is still faith toward God. So the attitude here is the attitude of faith toward God that puts the devil where he belongs. There is a constant perspective of God you must have in faith, no matter what you face, bearing in mind that the winning armour is not man's armour. It is the armour of God.

Many evils confront the [consistently] righteous, but the Lord delivers him out of them all. He keeps all his bones; not one of them is broken. Evil shall cause the death of the wicked; and they who hate the just and righteous shall be held guilty and shall be condemned. The Lord redeems the lives of His servants, and none of those who take refuge and trust in Him shall be condemned or held guilty…Psalms 34:19-22.(Amplified)

This testimony of a war veteran about God is that though the evil confrontations, rendered as afflictions or troubles in other versions of the Bible, are many, the deliverances made available and wrought by the Lord are equally many and even more. But how did he position himself for divine intervention in the face of all these evil confrontations, as we can see it was faith at work. Taking refuge and trusting in God is simply referring to faith at work. Since the troubles are many and diverse, the actions of faith taken will definitely be diverse as well. The only constant therein is the attitude of faith in the face of these many afflictions.

I would like us to take some trips to a few battle-grounds in the life of the man David and see how faith attitude enhances the faith shield in quenching all kinds of darts hauled at a man of destiny.

Scene One:

Identity Matters

It is difficult to talk of David's numerous battles in life and not mention Goliath. I know many sermons and vital lessons have been drawn from this passage, but a crucial one we must not let slip is the fact that David's faith attitude brought God on the battle field to kill Goliath.

And the Philistine said, I defy the armies of Israel this day; give me a man, that we may fight together. When Saul and all Israel heard these words of the Philistine, they were dismayed and greatly afraid…1Samuel 17:10-11.

The giant just roared from his depth of knowledge of history and warfare, and the people also reacted accordingly. Saul, a general, was also not found wanting in reactions. As far as Goliath was concerned, the battle was between two nations, and the combat he asked for was between him and whosoever. It was indeed a battle of realities.

And all the men of Israel, when they saw the man, fled from him and were dreadfully afraid. So the men of Israel said, "Have you seen this man who has come up? Surely he has come up to defy Israel; and it shall be that the man who kills him the king will enrich with great riches, will give him his daughter, and give his father's house exemption

from taxes in Israel."…1 Samuel 17:24-25.

If there were any iota of doubt in their hearts as to who they were fighting or representing in the battle, Goliath came again to clear their doubt for them. He made them realize his nationality and credentials and spelled theirs out to them as much as he knew, and the soldiers and their commander took it in, hook, line, and sinker to ignite the flame of defeat in their heart.

As far as they were concerned, the battle was a territorial battle, a battle between two sovereign nations represented by their armies, no more or less. In fairness to them, they saw the reward and sweetness that would follow victory if it could happen. Riches, status changed martially and otherwise were good and desirable but the reality of the victory never crossed any of their minds. Every human being wants victory in life, Christians in particular. Everyone would rather live debt free, sickness free, above and not beneath, but to many these are just wishes that never become reality.

Then David spoke to the men who stood by him, saying, "What shall be done for the man who kills this Philistine and takes away the reproach from Israel? For who is this uncircumcised Philistine, that he should defy the armies of the living God? 1 Samuel 17:26.

Goliath said he defied the army of Israel. Saul and his men said that was true. In contrast, David said no, it was not just an army of a nation called Israel, not just a territorial battle between two nations. It was the army of the Lord representing God in the battle between him and his enemy. We saw earlier in this book that the primary reason the wicked one fights you is because you belong to God. Saul, an older war veteran, a rich man indeed, could not even see beyond the human classification and nomenclature of his person and army.

David invariably was saying that this battle was not an ego trip to prove any point. It had nothing to do with the reward per say but a discernment of identity. Sure the army carried Israel's passport and flag but we belong to God. How many times have folks made a statement like what has God got to do with it. Even Christians say that when confronted with challenges. They totally forget that they were bought with a price and they belong to God.

Faith is not a show of strength. It is not a competition whereby you prove a point to your neighbour about who has more or who is the spiritual black belt. The foundational attitude in faith toward God is the sense of belonging, being conscious of his ownership over your life. If he owns you, he owns your body and health. He owns your purse, your career, and family. When there is any evil confrontation, you are conscious of who is being really confronted. Maybe you do not know God is a man of war. He is not just a man of war, he is strong in battle. This was the mindset of David before he took on Goliath. In fact, he was not fighting for God but with God and his declaration was that God himself would kill Goliath even though he knew he was the one who would aim and flick the sling and take the sword to cut his head.

Then David said to the Philistine, You come to me with a sword, with a spear, and with a javelin. But I come to you in the name of the LORD of hosts, the God of the armies of Israel, whom you have defied. This day the LORD will deliver you into my hand, and I will strike you and take your head from you. And this day I will give the carcasses of the camp of the Philistines to the birds of the air and the wild beasts of the earth, that all the earth may know that there is a God in Israel…1 Samuel 17:45-46.

Cooperating with the divine is easy once you are sure of your ownership. You will not leave what you ought to do for God neither will you lay claim of doing what God alone can do. No one in the army of Israel could take on Goliath, but someone in the army of God could and he did. It all boils down to your identity consciousness. Many are too conscious of their nationality and tribe, others of their beauty and stature. So many in the kingdom are too conscious of their social status that they would rather take that on in the face of conflict than their kingdom identity.

That the sharing of your faith may become effective by the acknowledgment of every good thing this is in you in Christ Jesus…Philemon 6

Effectivity in the school of faith is a function of proper identity mindset.

Faith lesson on mindset: You are not your own, you belong to God; trust him fight along because the battle of faith is the Lord's.

Scene Two:

Divine Presence Equals Divine Involvement

Experiences have shown that, though much support from outside may be available and is desirable in conflicts, life's battles are personal. Even though people support you, they cannot feel what you are feeling like you feel it. The temptation when the going is rough is to assume you are alone and on your own, especially when the battle is tougher or persists a little beyond your expectation.

David was anointed to be King as a teenager. The man he was to succeed was also anointed by same God, so a smooth transition would not have been out of place in David's expectation. In as much as he was not praying that the king die and would rather wait for his own time as ordained by God, being chased around in the bush and escaping the javelin by a whisker was not what he bargained for when he laid down his head for the oil a few years before. If life's challenges come to us the way we want them, when we want them, and for how long we want them, no one will ever mind being a life solider. But the reality is they do not come on our terms. They come with the intention of staying forever till they accomplish their mission to destroy us. No wonder the Bible calls them the fiery darts of the wicked one. If anyone should give up, a man who was not even living in the city where the throne was talk less of ascending it more than 10 years after his ordination qualified by all means. One day the tables seemed to turn to David's side and he had the chance to kill the king and be the paramount one finally. But his mindset took over, and he acted based on his belief system contrary to common sense.

So David and Abishai came to the people by night; and there Saul lay sleeping within the camp, with his spear stuck in the ground by his head. And Abner and the people lay all around him. Then Abishai said to David, "God has delivered your enemy into your hand this day. Now therefore, please, let me strike him at once with the spear, right to the earth; and I will not have to strike him a second time!"

But David said to Abishai, "Do not destroy him; for who can stretch out his hand against the LORD's anointed, and be guiltless? David said furthermore, as the LORD lives, the LORD shall strike him, or his day shall come to die, or he shall go out to battle and perish. The LORD forbids that I should stretch out my hand against the LORD's anointed. But please, take now the spear and the jug of water that are by his head, and let us go…1Samuel 26:7-11

This was the third time this scenario played out, but I chose this because of the profound light in David's words above. Bear it in mind David would not have minded if Saul had died. In fact, he knew that the battle was a matter of life and death. Simply put, it was David's life or Saul, but he would rather not do it by himself with the arm of flesh.
Why?

David said this man was anointed, so divine presence is with him, and once God is present, God is actively involved. David further said that the involvement of God in the matter was so active that God knew when and how to kill Saul at his own time. In response to this massive faith mindset, that was the last time Saul was able to pursue David. That was the day Saul's death sentence was written by a man of faith. The sequel of events from this point led to the death of Saul, if you read the passage further.

The anointing of the Holy Spirit was the abiding presence of God on the Old Testament saint given to them for assignment and yet David knew the implication that much. How much more now that the abiding presence lives inside of you. If God was involved with them being present on them for assignment, he is much more involved in your case now, being resident in you as his temple.

God is in you and so he is involved in your struggles. You have a high priest who is involved so much that he feels what you are passing through. He is as concerned as you are and desires that you win.

Let your]character or moral disposition be free from love of money [including greed, avarice, lust, and craving for earthly possessions] and be satisfied with your present [circumstances and with what you have]; for He [God] Himself has said, I will not in any way fail you nor give you up nor leave you without support. [I will] not, [I will] not, [I will] not in any degree leave you helpless nor forsake nor let [you] down (relax My hold on you)! [Assuredly not!]...Hebrews 13:5

God's presence in you is an indication of his commitment to you. With such a mindset, you are confident of his involvement no matter how fierce or how long the battle. If God is truly involved, which he is, you are sure of who will come out on top. Faith for you should stop being a struggle.

Faith lesson on mindset: You are not on your own, trust the greater one in you for victory.

Scene Three:

<u>God Is Always Right</u>

David did not just fight against kings and giants. He fought moral battles also, and David can hardly be mentioned without Beersheba, the wife of Uriah the Hittite not coming up as a topic. It was part of the fight.

And Jesse begot David the king. David the king begot Solomon by her who had been the wife of Uriah Mathew1:6.

Thousands of years after, the genealogy of Jesus had been narrated, the issue came up again. We shall see the significance later. This was a sore moral battle he fought. Even when it looked like he had lost it to a casual observer, David won. The same woman produced the lineage reckoned with by God as far as human redemption was concerned. The throne of David was established in eternity today on the platform of the lineage built through that woman.

To paraphrase what happened: David committed adultery with one of his soldier's wife, killed the husband in order to cover his sin, and had a son from the sad event. God pronounced judgement on David including the death of the son from this illicit act.

No doubt God is a forgiving God and David knew. He genuinely repented and God said He had forgiven him. The little boy fell ill, and David stepped up his prayer with fasting believing God would heal in his mercy. Alas, the boy died, so what would he show to the people as the token of the forgiveness he said he had obtained from God? Much gossip had been going on in the country about the backslider king who did an abominable thing. To merely fast and pray with sack cloth would have been a funny doctrine of procuring forgiveness as far as they were concerned. We know better and cannot be deceived, many of them would have whispered.

Having seen the impact of Saul's backsliding on Israel as a nation before, it was not impossible that military coup was on the way unless the ranks and files were sure the sinful king had been truly pardoned by the "no–nonsense God" they serve. You need to see the message Joab, the Chief of Army staff sent to David from the battle front shortly after this event to express the feelings of the soldiers.

Many religious zealots would probably have started postulating that the throne was jinxed, seeing that the earlier occupant also backslid. Maybe an envoy of concerned elders had been sent to the king reminding him of how fierce God's judgement could be on backsliders, how dangerous it was to still be on the throne with such an abominable record. I can imagine David thanking them for their concerns and assuring them that God had forgiven him. "Ask Nathan, the prophet," he probably would have said. The ones who saw or heard of how fierce Nathan was when he delivered the judgement would probably have concluded that part two of the prophecy that talked about forgiveness was born out of intimidation or gratification. Maybe he is afraid of stepping on toes or the king had given him something, they probably would have said.

"If God forgave you, why was the boy sick," they asked. "Yeah, just a fever but God will heal him," David answered. "Are you sure this is not the beginning of an epidemic on the whole nation," they probably asked. "Not at all, God will heal him," David said. "We shall see," they quipped. "The battle now is the dilemma of forgiveness, if we are forgiven why is the boy still sick?" Beersheba would have asked. So David was fasting and praying for healing of the little boy. He needed to prove a point of faith but the boy still died.

Once the boy died, David should have swapped position with God and become the judge. If truly you are merciful, where is the mercy? You said you have forgiven and we learnt you kept your word, how come you did not keep this? The judgement borne out of self pity and self righteousness could have stretched on with a threat of really backsliding, since repentance seems not rewarded. "Why bother, I cannot kill myself. Man has to be man," could have been his responses.

But when David saw that his servants whispered, David perceived that the child was dead: therefore David said unto his servants, Is the child dead? And they said He is dead. Then David arose from the earth, and washed, and anointed himself, and

changed his apparel, and came into the house of the LORD, and worshipped: then he came to his own house; and when he required, they set bread before him, and he did eat. Then said his servants unto him, what thing is this that thou hast done? Thou didst fast and weep for the child, while it was alive; but when the child was dead, thou didst rise and eat bread. And he said, while the child was yet alive, I fasted and wept: for I said, who can tell whether GOD will be gracious to me, that the child may live?

The summary of David's judgement on the matter was that God was right. It was painful but God was right. I would rather have him alive, but God was right. People may mock me, but God was right!

God was right because God is ever right.

The elders who thought David would pick a fight with God were astonished. They could not hold it. Shortly afterwards, David had another son, a token of triumph, through the same woman. While the elders were waiting for God to kill the new boy, too, God sent the prophet to say he was given the new boy out of love. If David had fought God thinking there was plenty seed in his loin, why bother about one God who cannot even forgive and forget. He would have missed the eternal opportunity of Jesus being called the Son of David. The God who killed the first could have aborted the second.

In this journey of faith, no matter the outcome, God is always right. Faith with this mindset goes beyond name it, claim it. It is a right disposition toward God person no matter what goes on in your material world.

Faith lesson on mindset- God is always right; even when you do not understand the concept, trust his judgement.

Scene Four:

God Is Ever Good

David did not only fight giants and other enemies, he fought himself and shot himself in the leg with help from Satan. He struggled with the pride of life and temporarily lost the battle but thank God for his goodness that endured forever. He went ahead and counted Israel, a nation God promised Abraham would be as countless like the sand of the sea shore. But a modern king would not have any of those old-school theories, and there he went breaching the covenant. God was angry with him and sent the prophet to him, highlighting the possible choice in judgements. David having come to himself saw only one viable option in the conflict of life. An angry good God is a zillion times better that a smiling devil.

And David said unto Gad, I am in a great strait: let us fall now into the hand of the LORD; for his mercies are great: and let me not fall into the hand of man...2 Samuel 24:12

Even when the justice of heaven demands that God comes down on you harshly, his bowel of mercy is never dried. They are new every morning, the word says. In divine chastisement is also a shelter of love. When you opened the door for the adversary as David did and the permissive will of God allows the adversary to have his way, know it clearly that the adversary was only able to do whatever he was doing because a door was opened for him through you. But also have it strongly in your mind that God is good and all he is thinking and working out for you is a way of escape. This will help you to position yourself in the place of help, where divine light can reach you and enable you come out of darkness.

Having done just the above, the Lord showed David by the hand of the prophet what to do to stop the pestilence.

And David built there an altar unto the LORD, and offered burnt offerings and peace offerings. So the LORD was entreated for the land, and the plague was stayed from Israel...1 Samuel 24:25

If all he was thinking of was how hard God was to please and how fierce his judgement was, the plague would have probably wiped out the whole city. You need to have it settled in your mind that God is good no matter what. God is not good because he does well in your rating. He is good because he is good and his mercy endures forever. When you mark God's answer script left and right, back and front, without any iota of doubt must you be able to judge him faithful like Sarah no matter what you are going through right now.

Through faith also Sara herself received strength to conceive seed, and was delivered of a child when she was past age, because she judged him faithful who had promised. therefore sprang there even of one, and him as good as dead, so many as the stars of the sky in multitude, and as the sand which is by the sea shore innumerable…Hebrews 11:11-12.

Sarah could have questioned divine motive: If God knew he would give me a son why not earlier when I was strong? Why not before another woman came into our marriage? Why not when I was be agile and alert to train him well? But she rather judged God faithful and good. By this token she received the strength to deliver her triumph.

Giving God thanks only when the bread has butter is unbelief. Even with a dry morsel on your table or no morsel at all, God is not less good to you than when the milk and honey flow like river. When the battle is fierce, have it at the back of your mind that the will and plan of the good God for you is ever good, the battle is for you to win. God is good, his motive is good, his plans are good, his promises are good, and his timing is good. You are in the good camp of life. Expect the battle to turn out good for you.

And we know that all things work together for good

to them that love God, to them who are the called according to his purpose...Romans 8:28

God factor in your affair is the good factor.

Faith lesson on mindset-: God is good no matter your experience, his mercy weighs than a tonne of sacrifices; when all else fail, in sovereignty lies bowel of mercy. In conclusion, real faith toward God is built on these four platforms:

(1) *That you belong to God,*

(2) *That God is involved as much as you are involved in this battle,*

(3) *That God is always right no matter what the outcome and*

(4) *That God is good all the way, even in his rebuke, anger or judgement.*

In warfare, if the darts coming at you seem too fiery or heavy for your shield, do not throw in the trowel and start running here and there. If you are serious and fully prepared for winning, all you need is a strong shield of faith. Develop it.

Your word depth determines your shield strength. The level to which you know is the level to which you will expect. When troubles rage and hope seems ebbing, separate yourself for more word encounter. The word cannot hit your spirit and not produce a ripple effect of faith for conquest. Even in sobriety and vigilance all you are trying to lay hold of is your shield of faith.

Be sober; be vigilant; because your adversary the devil walks about like a roaring lion, seeking whom he may devour. Resist him, steadfast in the faith, knowing that the same sufferings are experienced by your brotherhood in the world...1 Peter 5:8-9.

When faith is steadfast, the adversary will meet an insurmountable resistance and flee. Steadfast faith is product of steadfast word.

Yinka Akintunde

CHAPTER 07

UNDER DIVINE COVERING

Therefore, put on every piece of God's armour so you will be able to resist the enemy in the time of evil. Then after the battle you will still be standing firm...Ephesians 6:13 (NLT)

Put on salvation as your helmet...Ephesians 6:17a (NLT)

The phrase "every piece" in the passage above is not a mere numerical emphasis, it is the necessity of the whole armour being in place completely at all time. The ability to resist the enemy in the evil days is a function of how complete the pieces are in their every form and variety.

If every piece of the armour is needed for a successful

warfare in life, salvation being one of them cannot just be a mere escape route to heaven. Salvation indeed is the only guarantee for an eternal home with God hereafter, but salvation is also the guaranteed way of escape from hell and its attack while on earth. The reality is that even though the devil knows that by salvation through Christ Jesus you have escaped going to hell in eternity, he still endeavours to bring hell to you here on earth to make you feel the heat of eternal doom. That is why when things go really awful, you feel choked and life looks like a never-ending eternal torment of a kind, a misfortune not worth living. Salvation being the antidote of hell, therefore, is not just given by God to rescue you from eternal hell but also available for you as an armour piece against the scorching heat of torment from the adversary, even the devil.

Armour For Your Head.

Just as most fierce battles of life are fought in the mind or your head, so is the most hurtful pain felt in the mind more than anywhere else. The pain of unemployment is felt more in the mind than in the purse. The agony of a broken relationship may drain the purse and affect the look, but the weight and scar are on the mind. The seeds of suicide and psychiatric breakdown are only sowed in the mind even though the purse is the one suffering the battery. Satanic attacks through various media are set to mess up your head make you lose your mind and so your victory.

Life situations and experiences can be so bad at times that it seem like a hell hole, I have heard folks use that as a platform to dismiss the existence of eternal hell claiming that the heat of life's troubles here already passes for hell.

This is not true. What you feel here and call hell is just an onslaught from hell. When you are faced with all kinds of issues from hell trying to mess up your head, put on your helmet of salvation. It is God's escape route from hell to all who believe.

Before you contemplate suicide or giving it up all together and succumb to the force of hell, I need to ask you a pertinent question.

Are you saved?

If your answer is a yes, then to be saved is to have salvation, which can be taken up and donned as a cap to keep your head (mind) intact when everything seems to be crashing. Put it on as helmet so that hell can stop messing up your head, so you can think straight and see what a glorious victory Jesus bought for you when he died and rose again. Salvation is the ultimate in the history of mankind. It took care of the partition between you and God. It also defines the boundary between you and the devil, reinforcing your enmity with darkness. You need to see salvation beyond a state or status. It is a weapon, a weapon that can be taken as a covering for your vulnerable mind in time of trouble. Every time the situation is messing you around, like someone who just woke up from a slumber, say to yourself "come to think of it I am saved, therefore I am safe." The ultimate price ever paid in human history is that of your salvation. No price is too daring for heaven to lavish on your victory.

He who did not spare His own Son, but delivered Him up for us all, how shall He not with Him also freely give us all things?...Romans 8:32

All things in this contest include victory over adversity no matter how bad

Helmet Of Hope

But let us who are of the day be sober, putting on the breastplate of faith and love, and as a helmet the hope of salvation...1 Thessalonians 5:8

Another dimension has just been added to the helmet here - hope. The helmet of salvation is to keep you in hope, which brings within you awareness that as God's property, all will be well with you no matter what you are facing now. Once the hope of winning the battle is lost and is not renewed, an edge has been broken and the adversary allowed in. Keeping hope alive in your mind or head in the face of life conflicts is your responsibility and also a way of fighting the good fight of winning.

One of the reasons why God did not keep the fact that

you are saved away from you as secret is so that you may consciously develop hope, even the hope of salvation. Your mind set should be this - that if God did save me from the kingdom of darkness at salvation, he could not have abandoned me at their mercy in time of need. If God is unconcerned and would not mind the enemy doing whatever he would with you whenever he would, God would not have saved or rescue you from the kingdom of the enemy in the first place. You need to know that in the conflict of life, your father God is the umpire and he will not count three until you are the one on top.

When you are down, know in your mind that you are not out and the fight is not over just yet!

Joy For Your Soul

No matter how long the adversary seems to be on top, the bell will not go off until the position is reversed. Therefore let hope swell up inside of you producing outflow of joy in spite of the circumstance.

Behold, God is my salvation; I will trust, and not be afraid: for the LORD JEHOVAH is my strength and my song; he also is become my salvation. Therefore with joy shall ye draw water out of the wells of salvation... Isaiah12:2-3.

The above scripture is the language of a winner; when confronted with various challenges of life, not giving up to the adversary is hinged on you drawing strength from the hope of salvation, knowing that you are coming out, on top no matter how dire the battles. With this in your mind or head as helmet, you can sing the song of victory borne out of the fountain of joy within you.

Salvation goes beyond redemption from sin to deliverance from the effects and impacts of sin on mankind. Salvation, therefore, saves from sin, sickness, poverty, depression, suicide, oppression, obsessions and all form of evil that stems from the fall of man through Adam. Divine provisions for escape from the various impacts and effects of sin are what the scripture above refer to as the wells of salvation. The wells include a financial well to cure the dryness in your purse, the healing well for your body, relational well to heal the hurts, the well of wisdom to cure folly. These wells are various and vital. They are the channel made available by God who is the source and fountain of living water all by himself. As crucial as the wells of salvation are, it takes a deliberate and conscious effort of being joyful to draw the water they carry. Joyful necessarily does not mean happy. Joyful means to rejoice from within based on knowledge even though there are challenges. The knowledge is the fact that you know it will ultimately turn out for your good because the kingdom of light fights on your side. It takes a saved man to know such joy. Inside of you is the formidable kingdom of God or light that has never lost any battle to the kingdom of darkness, which you are now confronted with, for light shines in darkness and the darkness has never overcome it. The deposit of God's kingdom in you are righteousness, peace, and joy in the Holy Ghost. This joy is the joy of salvation, which means the joy that comes from your knowing that you belong and are a part and parcel of a kingdom that can never lose a battle no matter what. This gives you an edge over your adversary. This gives you the confidence to rush at the giant like David did to Goliath.

The helmet of salvation in the battle of life is the audacious hope of winning even when it does not look like it. This hope is manifest in outflow of joy with your shoulders straight and neck stretched. No depression, no lamentation or self pity even in the face of fierce battle because there can be only one winner and that is you.

The Lord Is Your Cover

And behold, there was a man in Jerusalem whose name was Simeon, and this man was just and devout, waiting for the Consolation of Israel, and the Holy Spirit was upon him. And it had been revealed to him by the Holy Spirit that he would not see death before he had seen the Lord's Christ. So he came by the Spirit into the temple. And when the parents brought in the Child Jesus, to do for Him according to the custom of the law, he took Him up in his arms and blessed God and said: Lord, now You are letting Your servant depart in peace, According to Your word; For my eyes have seen Your salvation Which You have prepared before the face of all peoples, A light to bring revelation to the Gentiles, And the glory of Your people Israel...Luke 2:25-32.

This was a short account of what transpired when the Holy Spirit led a man Simeon to the dedication ceremony of baby Jesus. The man here was not born again yet he said he saw the salvation of the Lord, knowing fully that no one was born again until Christ died and rose again. But Simeon said he had seen the salvation, even the salvation of the Lord. What did Simeon see and call salvation is the question.

The man Simeon did not just say whatsoever was recorded according to the dictate of his flesh or mind. He came by the spirit into the temple, so he must have spoken by the leading of the Holy Spirit, too. Simeon saw the child Jesus, held him in his hand, and called him the SALVATION. Simeon took Jesus the Christ child in his hand, a baby being dedicated, but what he saw was not a baby but the salvation. Hence we can conclude that Jesus was more than just a saviour, Jesus is the salvation.

Therefore when the helmet of salvation was mentioned, you are being told to put on Christ Jesus as a cover over your head. Just like a real helmet gives safety against vicious impact in an accident, so does Christ over you in life's ride. You need to be conscious of your cover as a Christian.

The husband is said to be the cover over the wife. The

cover is the stronger one, the one that evil needs to break through before getting to the covered. A helmet does not just come on people's heads. You have to consciously and with effort put it on yourself. I have heard saints shout; "I plead the blood of Jesus" umpteen times once a cockroach moves in darkness. I am not saying it is wrong, but truly blood conscious saints don't need that ritual borne out of uncertainty and fear in the face of troubles. They are conscious of their covering as Christ Jesus, which includes his flesh, blood, water, spirit and every bit of him. Everything of Christ including the blood is in your cover against all evil onslaughts.

Christ Jesus is the husband of the church, a member of which you are, so this automatically qualifies you for this covering, but marriage is by choice. To put on Christ as the cover over your head goes beyond a sticker on your door and car or cross pendant on your jewellery. Putting on Christ goes beyond confession, it is a submission. Coming under the authority of Christ is what makes Christ the Lord over your life. He is either the lord over all or nothing.

But the righteousness based on faith [imputed by God and bringing right relationship with Him] says, do not say in your heart who will ascend into Heaven? That is to bring Christ down; or who will descend into the abyss? That is to bring Christ up from the dead [as if we could be saved by our own efforts].But what does it say? The Word (God's message in Christ) is near you, on your lips and in

your heart; that is, the Word (the message, the basis and object) of faith which we preach...Romans 10:6-8.(amplified)

The word of God as revealed through Christ is what the Bible refers to as the presence or personality of Christ made available to you today. To put on Christ implicitly means to submit to the final authority of the word. Coming under the word influence in the face of attack gives you the helmet edge of protection against all impacts.

Come Into The Fortress

Not losing track of our context here, we need to bear in mind that the Lord is our salvation and we are admonished to put on the helmet of salvation in order to win. The curious question now is when faced with war, does our divine insurance policy have a certificate or code to show on demand. The answer is a resounding yes!

The name of the LORD is a strong fortress; the godly run to him and are safe...Proverbs 18:10(NLT)

If salvation is to be of any value in time of trouble, the name of Jesus has to be brought to the forefront. It is not a sign of exclamation, neither is it a religious slogan. When you invoke the name of Jesus in trouble, the salvation inherent therein manifests there and then for your safety. The name of Jesus was not a name agreed upon at a conference or world summit. It was a name God gave to humanity through the art of Christ's obedience to die the death of the cross for humanity. He obtained the name as an inheritance or right. It was not Mary or Joseph's idea of a good name for their baby boy.

Having become so much better than the angels, as He has by inheritance obtained a more excellent name than they...Hebrews1:4.

How did he obtain it?
He obtained this name through death on the cross. Even though he was called Jesus while on earth as man, the delivering and all-conquering power in the name was only released when he died in obedience to God.

And being found in appearance as a man, He humbled Himself and became obedient to the point of death, even the death of the cross. Therefore God also has highly exalted Him and given Him the name which is above every name, that at the name of Jesus every knee should bow, of those in heaven, and of those on earth, and of those under the earth, and that every tongue should confess that Jesus Christ is Lord, to the glory of God the Father...Philippians 2:8-11.

As you profess the lordship of Jesus over your life, every knee that wants to stand or war against you has a single destiny, which is to bow. The name of Jesus is the trigger point of saints' salvation. It is more potent than a gun. It will fix any disease or opposition and bring any towering wall to kneel. Christ our salvation, the helmet with which we are covered, does it through His name. The scripture above did not say the Lord is a strong tower, even though it is the Lord who saves and delivers from all troubles. The Bible rather said that "the name of the Lord is where the covering is in trouble."

What is the name of the Lord? Jesus is the name. When called, a tower of fortress is built round whatever you are calling him to. This is where religious folks and the unbelievers miss God. It sounds too simple to be real, but the name of Jesus is potent enough to deliver from all evil. When taken up like a helmet and used as a cover from the evil impact of hell, you will see the salvation of the Lord.

<u>Take It Now.</u>

We then, as workers together with Him also plead with you not to receive the grace of God in vain. For He says: in an acceptable time I have heard you, and in the day of salvation I have helped you. Behold, now is the accepted time; behold, now is the day of salvation...2Corinthians 6:1-2

This epistle was written to a Church of saved people, the church in Corinth, and we can see the admonition not to receive the grace available in salvation in vain. It is possible to stand in the centre of God's move and yet be passed by all the goods it has to offer. The day of salvation here is also the day of the Lord, which is today, when Christ Jesus is still available as the merciful saviour of all mortal. Such a time or day like this is the day of succour or help, the acceptable time God wants to help his people out of their trouble. But you need to know and make use of it else the grace available now be wasted or be in vain. The Lord will not conquer the devil again. He has done so once and for all. The victory is now packaged in salvation. The realm of salvation is the realm where Satan saw the biggest defeat of his life. The defeat is so profound that a loud voice, like that of an umpire, announced the victory in the court of heaven.

Then I heard a loud voice saying in heaven, "Now salvation, and strength, and the kingdom of our God, and the power of His Christ have come, for the accuser of our brethren, who accused them before our God day and night, has been cast down...Revelations 12:10

This is the clear picture of your true realm. The enemy has been hurled down, defeated, and paralyzed. Whenever he tries to bring hell to you on earth, consciously take the helmet of salvation. Stand tall as one who has seen the salvation of the Lord with hope in your heart, joy in your spirit, and the name of Jesus in your mouth. Every knee resisting you will soon start hitting the floor.

Your victory will manifest for all to see and you shall rejoice in the Lord your God.

CHAPTER 08

PRAYER IS IN YOUR ARMOUR

Praying always with all prayer and supplication in the Spirit, being watchful to this end with all perseverance and supplication for all the saints and for me, that utterance may be given to me, that I may open my mouth boldly to make known the mystery of the gospel, for which I am an ambassador in chains; that in it I may speak boldly, as I ought to speak...Ephesians 6:18-20.

When talking about spiritual warfare, what Christians implicitly mean most times is prayer. We need to clarify the issue here. Prayer is just one part of the whole armour of life's warfare. Answering one question in an examination with about seven compulsory questions is courting failure with all determinations there are. This is why it is possible to be a *"prayer giant"* and still be a life dwarf, which is not the will of God. Holding prayer in the right perspective is what makes prayer deliver what it promises, which is your availing victory in the face of conflicts.

It takes all manner of prayers to deal with all manner of issues we come across in life. Therefore, in prosecuting your warfare successfully against all odds in life, you need all the prayers there are, effectual and fervent for that matter. It is one thing to see prayer as a rite to be observed, it is another to see it as an effective amour in life's battles. The latter is the biblical expectation for saints.

You are to see prayers as a potent amour with which to maintain your stand against all the onslaught of the wicked. Prayer is a tangible force of the Spirit you need to hold in the right perspective. No wonder Jesus condemned the religious show off of the Pharisee about prayer thereby making it impotent and defiling that which is sacred and potent. Here, we see the Lord did not say public prayer is bad, but he said, the motive for such prayer was what defeated it and made it unacceptable before God thereby making the whole exercise of no significance. There is no joy in being a prayer warrior if all you do is war and don't win or that you may be seen of men as a spiritual giant in battle but in the inside you are a losing minnow.

Sourced From The Inside

Christian amour is not sourced from man but from God who is a spirit. It is therefore an amour made available for men who are alive in the spirit. The scripture above said all prayer to God and supplication should be in the spirit thereby telling us where the headquarters of our prayer should be. Many pray with everything and everywhere except in the spirit, which is wrong. What you are saying with your mouth is only as good as what is engaged with your spirit man. This includes your heart, soul, and spirit. How well you articulate your words is not as important as how connected your spirit and heart are with God's spirit in prayer. You can be very verbose and take a tone of a "prophet" in prayer. It does not move God or even the devil as it were. Remember Hannah was uttering nothing and yet saying everything, and so she got everything. It was such a drama that day in church in so much that Eli the priest took her for a drunk, but God heard her prayers muttered in the mouth but violently screamed in the inside.

And it happened, as she continued praying before the LORD, that Eli watched her mouth. Now Hannah spoke in her heart; only her lips moved, but her voice was not heard. Therefore Eli thought she was drunk. So Eli said to her, "How long will you be drunk? Put your wine away from you!" But Hannah answered and said, No, my lord, I am a woman of sorrowful spirit. I have drunk neither wine nor intoxicating drink, but have poured out my soul before the LORD. Do not consider your maidservant a wicked woman, for out of the abundance of my complaint and grief I have spoken until now. Then Eli answered and said, go in peace, and the God of Israel grant your petition which you have asked of Him... 1Samuel1:12-17.

Even if it meant sending a backslidden prophet who could not even see beyond the outward appearance of things, God could not resist a heartfelt cry of the spirit from Hanna.

Am I advocating silent prayer? Not by any means, but we need to engage our spirit in prayer before engaging our mouth, for God who will hear and answer is a spirit who lives in the realm of the spirit accessible only through your spirit. When the activities in your mouth supersede the engagement in your heart while praying, it's called the oblation of a fool -Ecclesiastes 5:1-2 - so reposition your heart. Binding the devil with your mouth while fearing him in your inside or doubting your authority within only leads to mockery and defeat.

And Jabez called on the God of Israel saying, oh that you would bless me indeed, and enlarge my territory, that your hand would be with me, and that you would keep me from evil, that I may not cause pain! So God granted him what he requested....1 Chronicles 4:10

The above scripture shows a short but passionate prayer of a man in distress who God heard and made to have his desired result. How did Jabez do this? He did not even change his name as he was still called Jabez after being made more honourable than all his brethren. We would have been told if he had acquired a new name, so the name was of little significance in the pursuit of destiny. God did not ask him to change his name like Abraham, Sarah, Jacob or Peter. Why? Because he (Jabez) needed no persuasion or awareness on what he ought to be or what God wanted him to be. He was the one who got discontented, desired a disconnection with the past and present thereby initiating the move for a changed future.

Asking them to change their names was God's way of having them disconnected from their past or present, which was either bad or not good enough. They either were comfortable with or are unwilling to detach from it, changing their names thereby made them to be conscious of and getting acquainted with who they ought to be. Therefore changing a name is not a fundamental Christian doctrine to be sat with and arguing about. We should not sit down with such trivia and start making an issue of nothing, chasing shadows instead of the substance of the abundant life in Christ. Not all who bear names that imply wealth end up wealthy. Not all who bear names that imply victory are seen walking in victory and dominion. Life is more than the name you bear. Stop chasing shadows.

Warring With Understanding

The secret of Jabez getting it right in his war against sorrow was that he had in place in his heart or soul a right and solid understanding of how things ought to be in his life based on the covenants of promises before going on prayer adventure. For Jabez, the situation of his conception and birth was immaterial, his name by meaning or implication notwithstanding. Prayer to him was a potent force of connecting with a God who had access to his past, present, and future at the same time, so Jabez called on God of Israel. He probably had a choice of calling on other gods or not even calling on any at all, out of apathy and bitterness. After all, what was the God of Israel looking at before he was born into a mess that was not his own making, but he still called.

He called on the God of Israel.

Who was Israel?

Israel was the blessed prince, the one who did not settle for anything short of divine blessing even when natural challenges and barriers kept him off the equation. The same Jacob called Israel was the son of Isaac.

And who was Isaac?

Isaac was the heir of promise, even the promise of God unto Abraham saying "I will bless you in blessing and everyone who needs blessing in all the families of the earth will have to find a connection through you," Jabez's family included.

This was the span of Jabez's understanding and so he went for it. He went for the blessing and link up with the promise channel of blessing through prayer borne out of understanding. In that promise also were divine presence, enlargement and victory over the enemy. So he took the total package before God in prayer and started invoking diving stamp of approval on it through supplication. There was a curse in Jabez's life but he did not go for a "special deliverance." All he did was to key into the antidote of all curses, which is blessing as it is written:

Christ has redeemed us from the curse of the law, having become a curse for us for it is written, cursed is everyone who hangs on a tree, that the blessing of Abraham might come upon the Gentiles in Christ Jesus, that we might receive the promise of the Spirit through faith... Galatians 3:13-14.

Without seeing Christ, Jabez knew that for curses to lose their grip on a man, blessing has to come upon his destiny. Praying with no understanding of God, your enemy, and even yourselves in Christ will enhance muddling things up, which will eventually lead to uncertainty with tiredness setting in and victory given up. The light of God's word shed within your heart is the basis of sound understanding, including understanding in prayer. When we are told to always pray with all prayer, be it interceding for others, supplicating to God or commanding the adversary with authority, it should be with an in-depth understanding in the light of the word with the Church age mind set.

In The Spirit

What does it mean to supplicate in the spirit? It was sufficient for Jabez to pray with understanding in the Old Testament, but that is not enough in our days. We need to pray in the spirit also. Thank God we can do it. The living part of Jabez's inner man was his soul, being not born again then because Christ had not died and resurrected to give man a new life in their spirit. At new birth, your spirit comes alive, so you are said to be born of the spirit. Praying in the spirit for you, therefore, entails understanding in your soul or heart and mystery of God head in your spirit. Jabez prayed with a sound understanding of God's will, provisions and promises as an Old Testament worshipper. Now is the time for true worshippers, whom the Father seeks and they will do so in truth (understanding) and in the spirit.

Jesus said believers would speak in a new tongue. The promise was fulfilled in the apostles who then testified that the promise is for everyone who would believe in Christ after them. To pray in the spirit is to pray in tongues or in the Holy Ghost. What does it matter? Is it really necessary, after all I can pray with my language and be content that at least I know what I am saying, you are asking.

For if I pray in a tongue, my spirit prays, but my understanding is unfruitful. What is the conclusion then? I will pray with the spirit, and I will also pray with the understanding. I will sing with the spirit, and I will also sing with the understanding...1 Corinthians 14: 14-15.

Did you see the resolute word of will there, showing us we should pray in the spirit? I **will** pray in the spirit.

When I pray in the spirit, what am I doing?

For he who speaks in a tongue does not speak to men but to God, for no one understands him; however, in the spirit he speaks mysteries...1 corinthians14:2.

Tongue is not a show-off unto men of how spiritual you are neither is it a weapon of intimidating others but a means to a divine end. When you speak in the spirit, you are speaking to God and you are speaking mysteries. We understand speaking to God at least but why or what mysteries are we talking about.

And He said to them, to you it has been given to know the mystery of the kingdom of God...Mark 4:11a

The mysteries are the mysteries of the kingdom of

God. In God's kingdom, the glory is concealed in mysteries. Even the defeat of Satan by the Lord Jesus was concealed in mystery, which made the kingdom of darkness to have dug its own pit of downfall and fell into it by killing Christ before even knowing what was happening. So when I pray in the Holy Ghost, I am actually releasing the mysteries of crucifixion and triumph of the Lord Jesus over the power of darkness. No wonder so much power to deal with the enemy is always released when saints pray in the Holy Ghost.

Wisdom For Conquest

When praying in the spirit, you are positioning yourself for two powerful weapons with which to withstand the wicked and its wile. One of these vital weapons is the wisdom of God.

That your faith should not be in the wisdom of men but in the power of God. However, we speak wisdom among those who are mature, yet not the wisdom of this age, nor of the rulers of this age, who are coming to nothing. But we speak the wisdom of God in a mystery, the hidden wisdom which God ordained before the ages for our glory...1Crinthians 2:5-7.

It takes the operation of divine wisdom to triumph over the lies of the devil. We were told not to let our faith stand on the senses and wisdom of man but in the power of God. This power of God is packaged in

God's wisdom for us to operate in so as to bring the satanic wisdom roaring against us to futility. When the devil in his cunningness (wisdom) goes about pretending to be a lion, you will be shown in God's wisdom how to resist him in faith to make him to flee. This divine wisdom is packaged in mysteries, and these mysteries are revealed to us by God through His spirit especially when we pray. It is like God decoding life unto you literally. When you pray in the spirit, you are speaking mysteries to God. This implies that God will be speaking mysteries back to you, too, in decoded form, which brings revelation or understanding into your heart of how to take delivery of your triumph. This is how human spirit encounters lights with which to silence the princes of darkness.

Power To Prevail

The Bible refers to believer as living stone, which means a stone that can grow. We are to be built up for divine habitation, a battle axe in the hand of God. Your access point to Christ is faith, as you are being built in him you are said to being built in faith. Christ our master was called a rock of offence, so are you in Christ but the fullness of your impact on whatever you fall upon is a function of how well built you are.

But you, beloved, building yourselves up on your most holy faith, praying in the Holy Spirit...Jude 20.

When you pray in the Holy Ghost, you are building yourself up, adding to your spiritual stature and thus stamina and weight with which to fall on evil as a rock of offence, too. I remember growing up in a family where means had to be prudently spent, and yet our parents wanted us to have at least the basic goods as kids. So at Christmas, we would go to a store called "Bata" (shoe store) to get Christmas shoes, but in order to maximize the funds, my precious dad would buy a size or two above my actual size knowing fully that I was growing rapidly. While my feet were still smaller than the shoes, he will fill up the space with old newspaper at the front. As the New Year went by, my feet would keep getting bigger until I would not need the newspaper stuffing anymore.

Just as your strength increases while growing in stature, so is the power made available for your spirit too increases as you are built up in prayer.

The earnest (heartfelt, continued) prayer of a righteous man makes tremendous power available [dynamic in its working]...James 5:16b

I know the coming of the Holy Ghost at baptism brought power into you, but it is praying in the same Holy Spirit that makes the power He brought available for your exploits. Prayer unlocks the fountain of power resident in you thereby making it available for your use. There is no point having a precious thing that is not available for use. This is always the case when saints are busy bragging about how powerful and anointed they are by the reason of the Holy Spirit baptism and yet the effect and the impact of the power are elusive in their lives by the reason of prayerlessness.

Speaking Forth In Prayer

To speak forth means to prophesy. Most of us think that to prophesy, you have to be in the office of the prophet, but no. Apostle Paul in I Corinthians 14:13a talking to the church at Corinth said all of them may prophecy, which means to speak forth or forth tell. The dimension of the prophecy people are familiar with is the foretelling of events ahead as it was seen predominantly in the Old Testament, but there is more to prophesying than that.

When God wants a change effected on earth He uses men, for we are the landlord here, glory to God! ***(Psalm115:16).***

In some cases, all he would want men to do is to speak forth and the word in their mouth becomes God's Word. All heaven and hell, angel and demons are then compelled to fall in place in fulfilment of such word.

This was exemplified in the valley of dry bone. ***Ezekiel 37: 1 – 10.*** It was God's will to have the bones live, it was His power that would make them live but He still said Ezekiel should prophecy first.

Did God have to do that?

No, but He chose to as he pleased.

Things written are meant for your admonition. Even though it is God's will for you to triumph and it is His power that will bring the triumph but your spirit and your mouth are still needed to put you on top and to effect the change you so much desire. As we can see in the first verse, he was caught up in the spirit of the Lord, which simply means he was in the spirit and he immediately started prophesying. Was Ezekiel just muttering silly fantasies off his own head? Not at all! He prophesied as was told or as he was inspired by the spirit. He was not there performing or stirring up false emotions. He was not prophesying to collect "special offerings" or "prophet seed." His motive and motivation was not filthy lucre or self aggrandizement. He prophesied as he was commanded in the spirit.

If you are carried out in the spirit by the Holy Ghost, which is already inside of you, and let him inspire in you what to say, you will soon start speaking change to situations of life and begin to see same change you are speaking forth, just as Ezekiel did.

Is it not funny that religious folks love prophesying doom and failure or how bad the situation is, but that is not the way out. God knew and saw that bones were very dry and all stood alone, but the Word of the Lord is always the healing word to bring the dry and straying pieces together in your life. Ezekiel needed the hand of the Lord or the spirit of the Lord to come on him and be carried out in the spirit before he could be inspired to prophecy. But you do not need such experience to effect the needed change in the New Testament experience. You have the spirit of the Lord resident inside of you now and can pray or speak in the spirit without being carried out. Remember the Bible said he that prays in an unknown tongue is in the spirit speaking already. No wonder the verse that follows started talking about prophesying. They both come on the same lane now.

Pursue love, and desire spiritual gifts, but especially that you may prophesy. For he who speaks in a tongue does not speak to men but to God, for no one understands him; however, in the spirit he speaks mysteries. But he who prophesies speaks edification and exhortation and comfort to men. He who speaks in a tongue edifies himself, but he who prophesies edifies the church. I wish you all spoke with tongues, but even more that you prophesied; for he who prophesies is greater than he who speaks with tongues, unless indeed he interprets, that the church may receive edification...1Corinthians 14:1-5.

While speaking in tongues, you are speaking to God, the same way it is possible for God to speak back in the words of prophecy for the people in public meeting for comfort and edification. Often God will give you the word of prophesy for yourself or situations round you to speak forth into while praying in the private. We were told that when such words come, they are better with the interpretation for complete edification. The word of blessings you understand encourages you better. Do not overlook words of prophesy. They are battle axe to war, a good warfare when the going is rough. **(1Timothy1:18).**

You also need to know that while praying, on many occasions, you likely do not have all of the information as to the reality of things as they are in realm of the spirit. This is referred to as weakness or infirmity, a kind of limitation you are subject to as human. How do you overcome such infirmity or limitation in prayer?

It is by the help of the Holy Ghost.

How does the Holy Ghost get this done?

By giving you utterances beyond expression of man's words, also referred to as praying in the spirit.

Likewise the Spirit also helps in our weaknesses. For we do not know what we should pray for as we ought, but the Spirit Himself makes intercession for us with groanings which cannot be uttered. Now He who searches the hearts knows what the mind of the Spirit is, because He makes intercession for the saints according to the will of God...Romans 8: 26 – 27.

Praying For Others

and for me, that utterance may be given to me, that I may open my mouth boldly to make known the mystery of the gospel, for which I am an ambassador in chains; that in it I may speak boldly, as I ought to speak...Ephesians 6:19-20.

It is also important to know that in life's warfare, your heart for the wellbeing of others counts before God. As a believer, you have been designated as a branch in the vine with many branches. You are to see to the nourishment of and bear the burden of other branches. You are a lively stone in the whole building. The standing of other stones in the building should be your concern if you truly have a heart for the Lord.

The above analogy shows us the reason why praying for others is a vital tool in your own standing also. Instead of migrating from congregation to congregation looking for special anointing to win the battle, you are rather admonished to pray for your man of God that the bold access to the mysteries that makes for your mastery be granted him or her thereby flooding the body of Christ with enormous light to banish darkness to where it belongs. Job was a man fighting the toughest battle of his life, having sustained many losses and suffering many bruises. Praying for others should be the last thing required of such a one. It is humanly unfair to ask Job to start praying for others who did not even suffer half of the loss he had suffered. They were not even as sick as he was. But not with the Lord. Job was still commanded to pray or intercede for his friends who never lost what he lost nor suffered what he suffered for his warfare to be accomplished.

And so it was, after the LORD had spoken these words to Job that the LORD said to Eliphaz the Temanite My wrath is aroused against you and your two friends, for you have not spoken of me what is right, as My servant Job has. Now therefore, take for yourselves seven bulls and seven rams, go to my servant Job, and offer up for yourselves a burnt offering; and My servant Job shall pray for you. For I will accept him, lest I deal with you according to your folly; because you have not spoken of me what is right, as my servant Job has. So Eliphaz the Temanite and Bildad the Shuhite and Zophar the Naamathite went and did as the LORD commanded them; for the LORD had accepted Job. And the LORD restored Job's losses when he prayed for his friends. Indeed the LORD gave Job twice as much as he had before...Job 42:7-10

Job fought the battle of destiny. He was the one to whom much was given and from whom much was required. His friends could do or say whatever they pleased, but Job, a man of destiny, could not afford to. There are many instances in your life, as a child of destiny, where even though you are the one wronged by others, you have to still seek the good of your adversary thereby putting yourself on a vantage platform of love by intercession. Love seeks the good of others not the revenge on others nor downfall of others. Love is not competitive. These three crucial areas are where wrong motives set believers up for defeat even before prayer is made. If care is not taken, the message of faith and dominion is painfully misunderstood so much that folks are in petty competition in the church about who is greater, more anointed, or stronger while many are out to prove points within the body of Christ no matter how irrelevant or trivial or who gets wounded.

As potent as prayer is, being an expression of faith, it needs love to work. For in Christ, nothing else works faith like love. **Galatians 5:6.**

You are admonished to watch thereunto.

Whereunto?

Prayer, of course, with all perseverance and supplication for all saints. It is a form of watching needed by all lest the thief breaks into the ranks of the fold.

Does that mean that praying for others does any good for me?

Oh, yes, it is part of your armour and includes praying for the men of God as well. Many blessings are missed because people pray for themselves alone and not for other believers, and this is wrong. Remember we were

told to put on the whole amour not just pieces of it, not the pieces we like but the whole amour if we want to be victorious all the way and all the time. When the armour is not complete, a foothold or an entrance is being created for the adversary to wreak havoc.
Can you imagine what not praying for your fellow saints means - a deficient amour!

I know a lot of us were taught only to pray against and not for others. Many are even in some terrible competitions with fellow believers, other denominations, and ministries in so much that they pray against their own brothers and sisters. All these things rob saints of their amour and cause many casualties.

Let's Clarify Issues:

If prayer is going to be effectual as a component of your victorious armour, you need to hold it in the right perspective and engage in it in the right way and with the right attitude.

For the rest of this chapter, I shall be clarifying a few issues on prayer as armour with you. We shall look at what prayer is and what it is not. It is also necessary for us to look at what prayer can do and what it cannot do for you.

Prayer is not a show of strength:

Prayer is an affirmation of your dependence on divine strength, which you actually wait upon in prayer, a demand on heaven for strength in times of need. If you are strong already all by yourself, there is no point waiting on the Lord in prayer again. Those who wait upon the Lord do so to renew their strength. This was why Jesus condemned the open show off in the display of prayer by the religious leaders of his day. He said their show of strength disqualified them of any other addition or reward from God. **Mathew 6:5.** This is the singular reason why many so-called prayer warriors are winning nothing in the real sense of life issues. Many are out to show off their spiritual black belts thereby intimidating brethren with all kinds of fleshly, spiritual-looking grandstanding, delving into all kinds of "spiritism" as they depart from the simplicity of the gospel of Christ. It is common to see folks conjure all kinds of vision and at times have their minds taken over by the devil to manipulate innocent and gullible ones with fear factor. For you, prayer is a way of obtaining and renewing strength from the Lord to mount up as eagle in order to win all the way. ***Isaiah 40:28-31; Hebrews 4:15-16.***

Prayer is not an exclusive gift given to a few:

Everyone ought to appear before God in Zion. One of the salient points of Christian faith is the fact that God wants a firsthand relationship and fellowship with everyone. No one can do physical exercise on your behalf no matter how much you pay them. There is a place for benefiting from intercessions and ministry gifts of other people, but the bulk in the school of prayer for triumph in life rests on your table. Stop running from pillar to post. Sit down and seek issues out in prayer by yourself. If you need partnership of others in prayer, that is fine, but be sure you are praying and developing a sound personal prayer life for personal development.

Spiritual exercise, prayer included, is designed to develop you as a person. Contracting it out is spiritual irresponsibility that leaves a Christian weak, undeveloped, and unstable. **Psalm 87:4** Contracting prayer out to others while you are busy running here and there leaves you a weak Christian in the face of battle. Appearing before the Lord is the secret of acquiring spiritual strength, and no one can be strong on your behalf.

Prayer ought not to be made to the devil but unto God

:

We commune with God but command the devil in prayer. You do not need to be in the place or attitude of prayer to cast or command the devil. Jesus cast many on various occasions when walking or while teaching. When prayer focus is on the devil, something is wrong. There is a place of dealing with the force of darkness while praying, but this should not be a dominant article of prayer for believers all the time. Jesus teaching a prayer pattern only mentioned evil, which is from the devil, once out of all the various bullet points highlighted in that pattern today commonly referred to as the Lord's Prayer. **Mathew 6:9-13.** The real focus of communion in prayer is neither the devil nor you. The real focus as taught by the Lord is "Our Father." Prayer is about God, and unto him but for us and our benefits.

We do not pray to Jesus:

You are expected to pray to the father in the name of Jesus. Even though Christ was in the Father before the world was formed, once he manifested here on earth as man, part of the humility of humanity he took on himself was the need to pray just like any other human person surrounded with infirmity is expected to do. He prayed to the Father. The whole of John 17 shows us prayer from Jesus to God the Father. Having divinity in human form with them, the disciples were always directing their entire request for divine intervention to

Christ, which he used to grant or prayed to the father for them. After death and resurrection, Christ ceased being a man and took divinity on again but said prayer from thence forth will be unto the Father in his name and not otherwise. So, we pray to God in the mighty name of Jesus with faith of a guaranteed response. **John16: 24 - 28.** The word "that day" here refers to the post- resurrection era, which is what we are in now. It is noteworthy for me to also say that you are not to pray to angels or pray in an angel's name. Jesus said in his name not in the name of Gabriel or Michael or any other name out there. We are not expected to pray to Mary either or any mediator for there is only one God and one mediator between man and God even the Lord Jesus...**1Timothy 2:5.**

Prayer will not replace obedience:

No matter how sacrificial or fervent, obedience is better than sacrifice. Truly the art of praying could be sacrificial, costing you time, energy, or any other pleasure. But in God's rating all sacrifices put together, prayer and fasting inclusive are not comparable in value to obedience. Praying without obeying the injunction that whatever your hand finds to do, you should do it with all your might will only end up in frustration and poverty. A praying wife who is not submissive or a praying husband who does not love his wife is doing nothing but putting sacrifice ahead while obedience to scriptural injunction is lacking. It cannot work. Same goes for sowing special seeds for anointed prayer while obedience is lacking. Victory will be missing. This is the reason why an article in Jesus' prayer pattern is the reconciliation of your way to God through forgiveness, but we need to know that asking for forgiveness while still in disobedience is like tempting the Lord thy God. **1 Samuel 15:22.**

Prayer will never take the place of personal responsibility:

Faith works when you work it. Prayer should strengthen you to take responsibility and not absolve you of it. Saying God will do it while you ought to do it is irresponsibility that will result in monumental failure. Asking God to do what he has empowered you to do already is monumental irresponsibility that will only result in monumental failure. For example, God loves and wants everyone saved, but until personal decisions and steps are taken by a sinner wanting to be saved, salvation remains elusive. There are people out there whose slogan is prayer whenever they are confronted with the need of taking definite steps, which had already being highlighted in God's word. For example, the word says let him who steals do it no more but let him work with his own hand not let him pray or ask to be prayed for if he wants a change for better.

Many nations are run by grossly irresponsible lazy-minded leaders plundering the resources of their nations and running to crusade grounds for prayer to solve the nation's ever-increasing problems. It does not work that way. Stop stealing, but sweat out your brain with tangible, creative, and productive hard work. National or personal prosperity will come. Prayer plus tithe and offering without sound productivity of your mind and hard work in your hand will only leave you in poverty or make you a robber! Prayer employs divine help but you can only be helped in doing what you are doing and not capable of all by yourself not what you are not ready to do at all. For example, the scripture says that God is the help and supreme force behind anything we are building as man, but the responsibility to build still lies with man. Even in warfare, the armour belongs to God but it will only work on earth when a man puts it on and works it. So you are admonished to take and put on the whole armour of God, not just praying for victory. **Hebrews 3:4**

God is responsible for answered prayer only when men take responsibility. Just like in football or any sporting game, holding hands to pray on the pitch when adequate preparations discipline with commitment is lacking in the team will only result in prayerful failure; thereby making a mockery of the Lord thy God through irresponsibility. The Lord thy God is not a native of any nation or country neither does he have respect of person or nation!

Prayer will not kill the devil or demons:

Demons are spirit beings only subject to the last or second death. Our assignment is to cast them. Growing up in a very religious part of the world, I have seen people bring their traditional mindset over to Christianity and ignorantly back it up with pseudo-spirituality. The devil and all the demons are spirit entities just like angels. They do not die like men, so asking demons to fall down and die can make you feel good but has no meaning or effect in the realm of life. Even when Jesus was asked by demons if he had come to destroy them ahead of time, all he did was to cast them out. The earthly bodies they were cast into (pigs) were destroyed, but Jesus in another scripture gave us a clearer picture of what happened to the devils themselves. They simply look for another habitation or roam till they get one. When leaving, he did not bother wasting his time on killing the devils. He gave us power to cast them out or forbid them from having influence on or inhabiting whatever you are involved in. Principally, what prayer does is to reinforce and put you in the absolute consciousness of your superior position over Satan and his kingdom thereby strengthening your faith in the authority bestowed on you by the Lord to deal with kingdom of darkness.

Prayer will not change God:

God remains the same yesterday, today, and forever in spite of countless prayer warriors who have passed through the earth. God cannot be manipulated or coerced by prayer. Prayer rather makes you align with the perfect will of God. Most of what we call the will of God is what he just permits because of the position or standing we have taken coupled with the activities of the adversary we are dealing with. Prayer is one of the ways to register our adjustments or change of standing and thus we trigger the manifestation of the perfect divine will. The question is why God permits them in the first place. He does so that in our challenge we can really pay attention to our standing and what we stand for and thereby outgrow the weakness being exploited by the adversary and be free from his wiles once and for all. For example, Job was a goodly and godly man in the Bible, but the fear factor made him prone and subjected him to a constant accusation by the adversary. He was in the hand and at the mercy of the devil until God allowed Satan to do his worst **(Job1:12)**. The devil was able to touch everything Job had fear factor for, except his very life simply because he didn't fear death **(Job19:25-27)**. At the end of the warfare, Job outgrew his fear, knew God better, and became a free man whose things the adversary could not touch again. The fear and ignorance window was shut for ever, so was Job free from attack forever.

If every time the enemy is planning an assault God jumps in to disallow him, even when we keep leaving an open door for him to have a foothold, we will never grow up into what we ought to be in God. Growth is one of the changes that lead to greatness. When God permitted the devil to touch Job's things, he reacted in various ways to the pain, but at last he went into the place of communing with God (prayer). There he learned the nitty-gritty of the warfare. He discovered how he opened the door for the enemy and how to keep it shut. Job came out of the closet a changed man. Once Job changed, his situation changed. This time around the enemy had no way of coming in again because of changes encountered in the place of communion with God. Job then had children who could not be killed, business that could not be ruined, and a body that could not be devoured by the angry devil again. The adversary did not stop going to and fro looking for someone to devour at any time even after the recovery. He was just too strong for the devourer this time around. God did not change because Job prayed. Job changed because he prayed, and the wicked could not touch him again. **Job42:1-5, 16.**

When prayer changes you, your change releases the goodwill in God's heart toward you and terminates the ill-will of the wicked devil.

Prayer is an expression of your heart:

Prayer is not a reading of some old creed or counting of some beads that has no relevance to what you are passing through now. Prayer is not saying things that are absolutely not applicable to your circumstance just because they are found in a prayer book. Hanna poured out supplications from the abundance of issues in her heart not from the abundance of religious cliché written in some book centuries ago. You need to also know that the pouring out of your heart doesn't necessarily have to be just another opportunity for requests. Heart-to-heart fellowship with your loved one should not be about request every time. Prayer, therefore, is a time to pour out the abundance of love and appreciation you have for God in your heart before him.

Even when you do not have material needs or requests, you still need to pray. The essence of prayer is the heart fellowship with the father

Prayer is a sacrifice:

It involves the investment of your time, your sweat, and other conveniences. By choice you are expected to let go of distractions and consciously create a regular prayer schedule around your life no matter how busy you are. Christianity is a call to offer your life a living sacrifice unto God. A main ingredient in this sacrifice is your prayer, which must ascend toward God regularly from the altar of your heart from your temple like the incense of the Old Testament. **Psalm141:2.** Just like the Old Testament priest could not outgrow the burning of incense and offering of sacrifices as long as the altar and the temple remained, you cannot outgrow prayer as a royal priesthood, too. **Leviticus 6:12-13.** One of your priestly responsibilities is to keep the fire on the altar burning forever. Jesus said every sacrifice shall be salted with fire. The fire you need for necessary salting against the decadence of life is made available on the altar of prayer.

Prayer accents divine will:

Rather than having your will and way by all means, prayer is the fundamental alter of saying "yes, Lord." It was on the altar of prayer that Jesus said yes to the death on the cross, thereby winning the battle against the power of darkness eternally. **Mathew 26:36-46.** Jesus did not just submit his sprit, soul, and body to God's will without a struggle. He said even though his spirit, which is eternal and born of God, was willing to do the divine will, the body, which of the earth born of man, rather than consenting is drawing back. The sure way to bridge the difference in the will of the spirit and flesh is by laying both on the altar prayer. When you study the word, you shall see the will of God. When you meditate on the same word, you will have a clear revelation or light from what you have seen through study within your spiritual man. But when you pray, you harmonise your spirit, soul, and body in accenting what light you have seen thereby releasing the power to walk therein. The unwillingness and inability to say yes to divine will is also referred to as infirmity in some passages. One of the help you receive in prayer is to overcome this weakness or infirmity through the help of the Holy Spirit...**Romans 8:21.**This necessitates praying in the spirit. When studying, meditating, and praying in the spirit becomes a lifestyle for you, it will be easy for you to enter the place of prayer with confidence, seeing and calling things the way God sees and calls them thereby being sure and commanding response from on high.

Prayer is an exercise of your faith:

Prayer is an expression of your confidence in the all-knowing and all-powerful God from which you are sure of response whenever you call. **1John5:14-15**. Confidence here is not boldface or a transient feeling but an expression of faith. When the Bible calls faith the substance of things hope for, confidence is the substantial part of that substance which you are expected to hold on to till the manifestation of what you hoped for comes. Just like the receipt of purchase you collect from the counter and expected to present at the delivery point for the good you paid for to come into your hand, confidence is the substance left in your hand when hope get transformed to faith. That is why you are told not to throw it away. **Hebrews 10:35-37**.

Imagine paying for goods in the store and throwing the receipt in the bin before collection just because you have been waiting so long. You will then realise that the waiting has just begun by the time they refer your case to customer service seeing you have now complicated a simple buying and selling procedure. Most delay and denial we see while supposedly walking in faith are due to lost receipts, even the receipt of confidence. It is not difficult to know when the receipt of confidence is missing. The prayer language changes from that of a victor to that of a victim who is uncertain and unsure of God answering. Prayer fortifies your confidence. It is also a sure way of expressing the confidence you have in God. The prayer of Elijah on Camel was a simple expression of confidence in a God who answered by fire, whereas the prophets of Baal lacking in such had to cut themselves and bleed to make up for what was lacking in them and their gods.

Prayer is a way of commanding divine attention:

Even though God's intent for you is good, divine pattern demands your prayer as the way of drawing divine attention to its performance.

For I know the thoughts that I think toward you, says the LORD, thoughts of peace and not of evil, to give you a future and a hope. Then you will call upon me and go and pray to me, and I will listen to you. And you will seek me and find me, when you search for me with all your heart. I will be found by you, says the LORD, and I will bring you back from your captivity; I will gather you from all the nations and from all the places where I have driven you, says the LORD, and I will bring you to the place from which I cause you to be carried away captive...Jeremiah 29:11-14.

In God's pattern, there are no accidents. When Moses thought his turning was accidental borne out of curiosity, the angel of the Lord made him realised that it was not but divinely orchestrated. He was asked to put off his shoes in acknowledging that the holy God was the one in charge on that ground and not a mere happenstance or freak of nature.

The tendency to think that luck or someone else is responsible for your wellbeing is not impossible. God therefore allows us to birth our glorious destiny in the place of prayer thereby creating the deep-seated awareness in your consciousness as to where the goods are from when they eventually arrive. When in prayer, you seek the attention of heaven in fulfilling the good plan of God in your life. One of the responses heaven gives is to start showing you what to do and how to do it in order to arrive at the good destination God spoke to you about. While birthing your destiny in prayer, it will become crystal clear to you and become part and parcel of your consciousness who is the source and performer, no matter who or what he allowed to midwife it. David said having looked upon many high places for help, he eventually realised that his help came from the Lord...**Psalm121:1-2.**

I am sure you know David was a man of prayer and thus a man of destiny.

Prayer procures angelic activities to your favour:

Not only are angels your ministering spirit, they are the carrier of good news from heaven. They excel in strength performing the word of God, which you are declaring and accenting as divine will in prayer. **Psalms 103:20.**

Notice that the verse did not say "Angels hearken to the word but to the voice of His word." Your duty is to voice God's word in prayer, and then the angels take over the performance. When Corlineus's prayer came before God for a memorial, angelic activities were sparked on his behalf. **Acts 10:1-6.** Daniel prayed to God and angels were sent to prevail on his behalf thereby stopping the mouth of lion and turned evil round for Daniel's good. **Daniel 6:10-28.** This was not a coincidence. On another occasion, a clearer picture that corroborates the issue is better painted.

At the beginning of thy supplications the commandment came forth, and I am come to show thee; for thou art greatly beloved: therefore understand the matter, and consider the vision...Daniel 9:23.(KJV).

Daniel's prayer provoked divine commandment for the much-needed angelic intervention. Praying to angel is idolatry, but the right prayer to God, voicing his word, will bring the excelling angelic activities into the scene of your life. They are sent to cater for you. **Hebrews**

1:14. Your prayer, therefore, strengthens your angels on your behalf; while the lack of it leaves them with nothing to work on to excel in strength.

Prayer gathers the cloud of light or rain on your life:

What comes from heaven on earth to bless when men pray is likened to rain, and a man receives nothing except it be given him from above.

Ask ye of the LORD rain in the time of the latter rain; so the LORD shall make bright clouds, and give them showers of rain, to everyone grass in the field...Zechariah 10:1. (KJV)

One of the responses of heaven to your prayer is the release of a bright cloud or what I call the cloud of light. This is what dispels the cloud of darkness hanging over your head and gives you the lightness or freedom you need from heaviness. The reason people go around with heaviness in the kingdom is because the cloud over their life is void of brightness. You cannot be in touch with the kingdom of light in you on a consistent basis and still be carrying heaviness of heart around. Heaven looks like a ceiling of brass over many because they have not prayed down the bright cloud. In God's presence is the fullness of joy, which means joy incomparable to what anything else can give you is in the place of prayer. Why then are you depressed and dejected for so long? Someone can be in church and not in touch. One can be present in the assembly but yet be far from the presence of God. Judas Iscariot committed suicide not because he was not present in the group but because he was absent in the presence, so the joy was soon dried up by 30 pieces of silver and, phew, he jumped!

The rain of blessing is always preceded by the cloud of brightness from the Lord, and Jesus said the sure way of being given is to ask. There is asking in prayer, which commands a release from on high upon your life. The rain is meant for every grass, which means that there is no aspect of your life on Earth that the rain from heaven as response to your prayer cannot touch.

Prayer is a sure way, therefore, out of dryness.

Prayer dispels the cloud of darkness round you:

The prince of Persia constituted a thick cloud of darkness over Daniel's territory so that revelation could not flow, but persistent prayer weakened and dispelled it eventually.

Then he said to me, "Do not fear, Daniel, for from the first day that you set your heart to understand, and to humble yourself before your God, your words were heard; and I have come because of your words. But the prince of the kingdom of Persia withstood me twenty-one days; and behold,

Michael, one of the chief princes, came to help me, for I had been left alone there with the kings of Persia. Now I have come to make you understand what will happen to your people in the latter days, for the vision refers to many days yet to come...Daniel10:12-14.

Even though an angel did the fighting in the realm of the spirit, someone represented the kingdom of light in the realm of life here in the person of Daniel and until he fought in prayer on earth no angel fought anything in the spirit. The kingdom of darkness is a lawless aggressive kingdom. It was built on rebellion and lies from the beginning. It takes the armour of light to dispel its resistance and advancement. Your consistent and persistent prevailing prayer, like Daniel's, is a sure way to do that.

The earnest (heartfelt, continued) prayer of a righteous man makes tremendous power available [dynamic in its working]... James 5:16b (Amp).

One of the effects of the power spoken of here is the power to dispel the cloud of darkness engineered by the kingdom of darkness to prevent the blessing released from on high reaching you. Praise God you can do it in prayer!

Finally on prayer, when every other thing fails, prayer will procure for you the divine help you need in time of need. Whether against self or Satan, it takes the mercy and grace of God to successfully prosecute a battle in life. Such grace or help is always awaiting you as you pray.

For we do not have a High Priest who cannot sympathize with our weaknesses, but was in all points tempted as we are, yet without sin. Let us therefore come boldly to the throne of grace that we may obtain mercy and find grace to help in time of need...Hebrews 4: 15-16.

May you receive enough strength as you approach God's throne of grace in prayer, obtaining grace and mercy needed as help in this time of need for yourself and fellow saints.

I see you moving forward, winning life's battles from victory to victory in the precious name of our Lord Jesus, Amen.

Yinka Akintunde

CHAPTER 09

HE THAT WARS

No one engaged in warfare entangles himself with the affairs of this life, that he may please him who enlisted him as a soldier...2Timothy2:4.

In concluding this book, I want to reinforce certain salient points with you about life's battle.

First, the battle of life requires your active engagement. No one fights by proxy in life. You are expected to take the bull by the horns and actively get in the battle line in any area you sense the wiles of the wicked at work.

Winning is never by wishing. Many wishers litter the kingdom but champions' reckoning is only by engagement.

Life battles are not fought on the sofa in front of a flat

screen with a bowl of popcorn and ice cream or on the Internet, criticising everyone and everything. These are the unfortunate full-time engagements of many believers today in the name of Christianity. Many wrongly assume that winning an argument on social networks is the same as winning personal victory in the battle of life. It is therefore easy to see commentators and analysts in the body of Christ who can diagnose what is wrong with everyone and everything but themselves. They presume fighting for the faith, yet we can't see personal victory in them. The truth is, they are fighting the wrong battle with the wrong armour therefore getting the wrong results.

Second, you are to fight as a free man. Your calling is a calling unto freedom in Christ. Do not get entangled with the affair of this world again. One of the main causes of defeat in life's battle is distraction by entanglements. The adversary knows you are unstoppable if focused. He therefore brings entanglements across your way like a spider hunting a fly. The distractions range from legitimate daily needs to pride of life. Once anything gets in your way of functioning in your God-given armour, it is an entanglement. Like Jesus said, cut it off. It could be peer group, personal choice, a mindset you have kept for long or even seemingly spiritual activities. If it depletes your engagement in the real battle which guarantees your glorious destiny, get it off your back. Religious activities are an easy trap against real issues. The Galatians church was foolishly trapped in it at once, so the need for this admonition.

Stand fast therefore in the liberty by which Christ has made us free, and do not be entangled again with a yoke of bondage...Galatians5:1.

It requires standing to fight and win. This scripture says you should stand just like our anchor scripture, too, admonished you to withstand having done all to stand. Your standing fast against entanglements enhances your standing against all the wiles of the devil.

Third, your warfare requires endurance. The battle front of life is not meant for softies. Because of the wrong expectation for the easy way out of life after conversion, many believers have been sorely disappointed blaming not just the devil but everyone including God for what they perceive to be divine indifference to their challenges. Having given one special offering or making some spiritual sacrifices or being involved in kingdom activities of sort, many just expect the roads to be opened, the goods to be flying in, and life to be one jolly good ride with no roughness on the road. This is a wrong assumption with no scriptural basis. The reality is God is not blind to whatever good you do toward him or his kingdom, but you still need some level of endurance as his good soldier.

You therefore, my son, be strong in the grace that is in Christ Jesus. And the things that you have heard from me among many witnesses, commit these to faithful men who will be able to teach

others also. You therefore must endure hardship as a good soldier of Jesus Christ...2Tomothy 2:1-3.

If we are in for picnics, you will not be told to be strong. You do not need strength to watch television or eat ice cream! Do you?

You only require strength when the task is demanding. You are in a war that demands from you some inner strength and absolute endurance. The reason you need to endure is so that you may still be on ground when the manifestations of your victory arrive because they shall surely come. Many have vacated the battle front by the time their victory arrives. If God is not sure you will win, he won't ask you to endure. Your endurance is not just to get battered here and there for nothing. Your endurance is an art of holding on in battle because of the certainty of your glorious victory.

There is no point enduring if you will not win, therefore fight to win. To fight a good fight is to fight to win, not to lose.

Listening to some folks, you can see that all they are waiting for is losing. They always have an example of someone who was not healed whenever you talk about healing or someone who ended up losing the job even though a tithe payer or someone who had one calamity or the other despite believing God for victory. They are never comfortable with victorious or winning words, but when they hear defeatists talk spiced with unbelief, their day is made. The theology is correct, and the doctrine is pure and heaven bound!

If all God is seeking is for you to lose, he did not have to send Christ again anyway, knowing full well that all have lost in Adam at the fall in the first place. Christ came and blazed the trail of victory for you. He won the fiercest of all battles so you can win whichever one you are facing, too, in taking the spoils of the won battle.

Finally, you are in this battle to please God who is your commander in chief who enlisted and equipped you as a soldier unto victory and not defeat.

You did not enlist yourself. You were pre-ordained for victory by God, called through Christ Jesus by salvation unto justification, and equipped with the Holy Spirit for glorification.

Take up your armour and walk in victory unto which you were called!

Peace.

Yinka Akintunde

www.ingramcontent.com/pod-product-compliance
Lightning Source LLC
Chambersburg PA
CBHW032111090426
42743CB00007B/313